The Legacy of Starseed Wisdom

"Desley Lock is a gifted sensitive Starseed who resonates with multiple dimensions to illuminate and understand the mystery of experience and truth. Desley brings pure love to help others in their seeking."

Faunia Smith, Faunia Smith Art

"My inquiring mind began to research further into our galactic connection…" In this book, Desley Lock does a beautiful job of describing her life journey as it threads through varying levels of the multidimensional realities. Her experiences with ascension and the remembrance of her galactic family remind us all that we are truly from the stars and we absolutely were put on this Earth at this time for a reason.

This book describes in detail many of the Starseed lineages that Desley is aligned to through her astrology chart, the blueprint of her soul. Her shared experiences of awakening to the inner knowingness that she is a multidimensional being will remind us all of our unique light signature we are here to imprint on humanity.

Donna Diane,
Lightworker and Starseed Astrologer, Celestial Blueprint

To my darling daughter, Cherish. Thank you for coming along on the journey with me. Together our innate ability to resonate with the unseen has enabled the story of our prior Starseed existence to unfold.

Dear little Pearly Lock; my friendly shadow of fourteen years – always by my side – has entered the wardrobe for the very last time.
Forever in my heart.

The Legacy of Starseed Wisdom

Awakening pure potentiality to other realms of existence

By
Desley Lock

The Legacy of Starseed Wisdom:
Awakening pure potentiality to other realms of existence

Author – Desley Lock

© Desley Lock 2022

www.desleylocknaturopath.com.au

This book is sold with the understanding that the author is not offering specific personal advice to the reader. For professional advice, seek the services of a suitable, qualified practitioner. The author disclaims any responsibility for liability, loss or risk, personal or otherwise, that happens as a consequence of the use and application of any of the contents of this book.

All rights reserved. This book may not be reproduced in whole or part, stored, posted on the internet, or transmitted in any form or by any means, electronic, mechanical, photocopying, recording, or other, without permission from the author of this book.

Editing, design and publishing support by www.AuthorSupportServices.com

ISBN: 978-1-922375-22-3 (pbk)

 A catalogue record for this book is available from the National Library of Australia

Acknowledgments

Jean Sheehan (Millennium Education) – Your guidance and steadfast belief in 'shining my brilliance' inspired the confidence to write this book. Finding you and experiencing your courses revealed the ancient wisdom and knowledge kept hidden from me for so long. I am eternally grateful for your help in breaking down the barriers and releasing the negative patterning that held me back. **No more playing small.**

Donna Diane (Celestial Blueprint) – Thank you from the bottom of my heart for providing the knowledge of my Starseed lineage. No words can express my profound gratitude and joy at finally being able to solve the mystery of who I am.

Faunia Smith (Faunia Smith Art) – Your amazing intuitive art has captured the very essence of what this book is all about. Thank you so much for your unique insight into my Starseed experience and your mesmerising portrayal of my adventures into the higher dimensions.

To all the teachers of spiritual knowledge who have touched my life throughout the years: You have expanded my inquisitive mind in so many ways in helping me to reach my greatest potential each and every day.

To family, friends and my fur babies: Blessings for your unconditional love and non-judgemental acceptance of my way of being in the world.

To Alex, Margie and team from Author Support Services: Thank you for your patience and understanding while making changes to the manuscript. To be allowed to express the writings in my own unique way is appreciated.

Foreword

You know how sometimes you meet someone and you know in your heart that this person has profound wisdom to share with the world?

That is what I saw in Desley Lock.

I still recall the first phone call I had with her. She called to enquire about entities or ghost-like things in her house and what she could see. Straight away I had a connection as I have always been able to see these too but call them DUDES! The more she talked the more I knew she could communicate with the dudes and that she had profound knowledge to share with the world.

As we spoke, I saw an energy of her speaking on stage, talking to groups and writing a book.

Desley, thank goodness you followed through with this book!

It was when Desley started studying with me, learning my accredited Millennium Modality® – Medical Intuition, that things unravelled, and I witnessed Desley really share her insights and wisdom. As she learnt, or shall I say re-remembered, the aspect of all things galactic, beings, dudes, stopping time and the quantum, this was a perfect opportunity for me to say "Desley, it is time. You need to teach. People are ready."

It was at my Shamanic Modern Medicine Woman event and undertaking the Journey process that I could see her book coming to fruition. I loved listening to what she knew and how she saw the dudes in her house. I loved how she was now more comfortable saying what she could see and know.

If you have this book, no matter which way it came to you, you know that you are meant to connect with the gorgeous Queen High Priestess Desley. Her humble nature allows you to blossom as she teaches her knowledge. She is an outstanding authority in this field and has come to Earth at this time to shine the light on those that need to wake up.

And for some of you, it is a coming home and peace in your mind and heart.

Desley, years ago you were fearful to share, and many might have thought you 'crazy'. NOT ME! I knew then and know now that you know the truth of what needs to be taught.

Shine, my lovely Queen High Priestess.

And for you reading this book, whatever Desley offers – book in.

So much love and gratitude to you, Desley.

Jean Sheehan

Director Millennium Education – known as the 'Walking Talking MRI' Medical Intuitive

Preface

From the moment I was born I struggled to fit in. A sickly child with extreme sensitivity to noise and overwhelming situations I felt an enormous sense of not belonging and being different to others. From an early age I would feel a sense of homesickness for somewhere else which was hard to put into words but it would leave me with an incredible sense of aloneness. Although I made friends, due to my extreme shyness, I was often bullied and singled out by teachers for being different.

Although my sensitivity sometimes appeared as a curse and a weakness, it also provided the most exquisite way of experiencing the world. As a little girl, I could sense the spirit realms and was therefore able to delight in the smells, textures and tastes of the natural world in its entirety.

Growing up on a farm I was exposed to pesticides which led to suffering from rickets, sometimes known as soft bones. Despite exposure to sunshine my ability to absorb Vitamin D was compromised. This led me on a journey into the world of natural medicine. I was successfully treated by a naturopath who inspired a desire to be of service in the healing arts. In 1993 I graduated as a naturopath, with further university studies in 2018.

My ability to sense the paranormal has continued throughout my adult years. I have a deeper understanding that there is more to the world than I had been led to believe from religious and educational institutions. As a young adult I began having unworldly experiences which were difficult to understand. I have always had an interest in spiritual matters and am an avid reader of such material. However, the more I opened my mind to such possibilities through meditation and other rituals, the more my personal experiences became my reality. From sleep paralysis, speaking in a strange language in my sleep, creating resonance in my hands with water and electricity and telepathic communication with deceased loved ones, I shrugged it all off as just me being a bit weird.

As the years went by, a series of financial disasters, relentless bullying in work environments and relationship issues took their toll. I could no longer accept the harshness of the world as I began rapidly to spiral into lack of joy, even into despair. I had a complete breakdown in 2011 or what is known in spiritual terms as The Dark Night of the Soul. The ascension, or raising of human consciousness, had begun and it was time to wake up to the real reason I incarnated onto this earthly plane.

A series of debilitating physical symptoms and a prophetic dream of a gigantic weather event in my local area led to even more woo-woo disturbances. However, I was not prepared for what was to follow when paranormal happenings became extra-terrestrial activity.

I had never entertained the concept of originating from the stars, having only ever read about ghostly apparitions and life after death experiences. But when my house became the portal for close encounters of the third kind, I was forced to consider that something more than just a demonic haunting was trying to communicate a much more profound message. As more and more clues were left for me to unravel, I finally put all of the pieces of an intriguing puzzle together and ultimately arrived at the true origins of my existence.

Contents

Introduction	1
CHAPTER ONE : Starseed Childhood Sentience	3
CHAPTER TWO : Special Qualities of the Starseed	17
CHAPTER THREE : The Dark Night of the Soul – the Awakening Begins	35
CHAPTER FOUR : The Illusion of Reality – the Dragon, the Lion and the Shaman	47
CHAPTER FIVE : The Shamanic Way	59
CHAPTER SIX : Interdimensional Travels and The Jean Effect	73
CHAPTER SEVEN : My Starseed Origins	83
CHAPTER EIGHT : The Puzzle is Complete	91
Conclusion	107
About the Author	109
The Butterfly Connection	111

Introduction

This book is also written in honour of the ancients who are here to guide us, and to the many Starseeds who are weaving their magic of unconditional love and all-encompassing acceptance. It is also hoped that these writings shine a light for others who are struggling to find their path of belonging on planet Earth. May they also come to know who they are in their own time and their own way.

Do you:

- ★ *Ever describe paranormal experiences or visitations from alien beings that make you question your sanity?*
- ★ *Experience a deep feeling of wanting to go home, but are unsure where home is?*
- ★ *Exhibit characteristics of pale skin, low body temperature, reddish tinge to your hair and even an extra appendage?*
- ★ *Struggle in a world that seems to lack empathy, joy and compassion?*
- ★ *Intuitively know about people and situations before they occur?*
- ★ *Have RH negative blood?*

Then this book is for you!

CHAPTER ONE

Starseed Childhood Sentience

Starseeds: What are they and what is their purpose here on the earthly plane?

We are all ultimately made up of the same stuff as stars. However, there are some of us who have not only had many lifetimes here on Earth but also the celestial heavens. Our origins may be traced back to the sky people. These interstellar beings came from other star systems, planets and galaxies many thousands of years ago. They ultimately seeded a hybrid race of human alien beings which formed part of the new ancestral lineage.

My own journey has led to the discovery that I am one of these beings. What has brought me to this conclusion began from the moment of my birth and my sentient approach to being in the world.

I was born in a small country town in Queensland, Australia on 30 September 1961 (30+9+1+9+6+1 = 9+2 = numerology number 11) to a small crops and orchard fruits farming couple. What is my connection with this number 11? What does it mean to me? This birth number has played a pivotal role throughout my life and continues to do so today. Read on to find out why.

The last of six children, my soul was not happy to be delivered to Earth. I screamed endlessly and only a few weeks after birth became ill with what they called 'a germ in the bowel'. I was not expected to live and a Catholic priest offered to give the last rites as long as I was baptised.

I survived but continued to scream – endlessly. Most of the populace cannot remember being in the cot at under twelve months of age, but for me it is still as vivid as it was over sixty years ago. I had a small pink blanket with little scalloped-out holes in the knitting that became entangled in my tiny little pinkie toe. I found this sensory experience very irritating and would sob and cry for my mother.

That blanket was soon relegated to the op shop, but years later I asked where it had gone. I described it in detail to my mother, only to be told that I could not possibly remember it as, "You were only a baby."

As I became a toddler, sensory overload – an oversensitivity to noise and a total fear of strangers – made my life very difficult. No-one could get close to me except my mother. I would hide up in the wardrobe to get away from the relentless kisses from aunts and uncles. My senses were permanently heightened – mosquitoes sounded like freight trains and at night time, when the lights were out, people in pictures on the walls seemed to be trying to communicate with me. They would gesture with their hands and move their mouths as if trying to speak to me. I could not grasp what I encountered as the room was pitch dark, yet I could see the moving figures in the paintings. All I knew was it frightened the hell out of me. I would run through the house screaming that they were after me.

It was then that I experienced my first ghostly encounter. It was an apparition of an elderly man – toothless and dirty – who would huddle underneath my sisters' double bunk bed at night. I slept across from them in a single bunk and when I turned onto my side and looked on the floor, underneath the lower bunk there he was: As clear as day, even though it was pitch black. To my mind he was joking around by putting lighted cigarettes in his mouth, holding them for a few seconds and then pulling them out with a huge puff of smoke. I could see the cigarette smoke as it wafted up from beneath the bed. I would stare, transfixed, as it seemed he was trying to speak to me telepathically. I would then become terrified and, once again, would run through the house waking everybody up. This would not only disrupt the sleep of my disgruntled parents but fuelled the increasing resentfulness of my siblings. They found what they considered my attention-seeking antics frustrating and implausible. Little did I know that this extreme sensitivity to my surroundings would continue unabated throughout my childhood and on into the future.

In fact, the man under the bed turned out to be a homeless man who, many years prior to my father purchasing the house, had entered the then unoccupied home and lit a fire to try and get warm. Whether from a stray cigarette or an unattended fire, the house partially burnt to the ground resulting in his death. I first learnt of the homeless man when my mother became terminally ill and my father and I were discussing death and the afterlife. Imagine my surprise when I realised the apparition huddled under the bed during my childhood, had been a real person in a different lifetime but was ultimately stuck between worlds.

Were you a sensitive child with heightened extra-sensory perception (ESP)? This may be one of the signs to look for when describing a Starseed. Many of these children are born with heightened sensitivity and gifts of clairvoyance, clairaudience and clairsentience.

As I grew and became a young girl, I began to get a deep sense of not really belonging and wanting to go home to a place I could not define. My siblings found my sensitivities most annoying, as if they somehow sensed that I was not part of their tribe. Being a gentle soul who did not fight back, I was often the brunt of their pranks.

I had bowel problems as a baby. I did not digest food well and as we were relatively poor, if there was nothing to eat, we lived on fruit which exacerbated my diarrhoea. We relied on the old thunderbox that sat a fair distance from the house. The outhouse stank like nothing on earth and the seat would often be covered with spiders, blowflies and other creepy crawlies. Night-time visits meant you always took a torch to check the surroundings before you sat down, and the hard seat made it particularly uncomfortable to relax and concentrate on the deed. Whilst perching and straddling so that I would not slip down into the abyss – I heard a deep, animalistic voice screeching, "The bogie man will get you." The bogie man was considered some sort of demon and you wanted to stay well clear of him.

I grabbed my dropped daks, heart pounding, and bolted. I hoped to fall into the arms of a sibling. Alas, there was no-one there and, in my haste, I dropped the torch, leaving me in total darkness. The grass began to rustle and a shadowy figure emerged, again shouting, "The bogie man is coming to get you."

I screamed and screamed, and ran for my life. I tripped, fell and gashed my leg. I waited for the bogie man to devour me. Next, I heard a raucous laugh as the figure shone a light on me as I lay trembling.

"Cry baby! That'll fix you," the scornful voice said. I realised the monster was one of my brothers who seemed very pleased to see me in such discomfort.

Strangely, I never felt angry towards my tormentors, just a deep sense of isolation because I was not accepted.

It took a lot to ruffle my feathers, but I had become incensed when my brothers and sisters claimed that my doll, Candy, was brown because she fell down the dunny. This infuriated me. Why would her skin colour be unacceptable, even for a doll? I have always felt a deep sense of injustice that a story had to be concocted about how she became that colour. Again, these are clues to attributes of the Starseed generations. There is a strong feeling of disconnect from the family you have been born into. We are always seen as the black sheep who never quite fits in. We sense injustice from a very early age but have to sustain our compassion for others, even when ridiculed for being too sensitive.

Speaking of sensitivities, a Starseed nervous system is a highly tuned instrument. Any change of routine or emotional upset would result in my having bowel and bladder issues, nausea and sometimes vomiting. So much so, that childhood holidays were nightmares for me as I endured marathons in the old Vanguard car. It was always piled high with luggage and we kids were squashed in the backseat like sardines. Sometimes it took a couple of days to get to Ballina and even longer if travelling to the Gold Coast. The car would overheat and we would often have to stop for the engine to cool.

I loved travelling in the car, particularly at night when the reflection of the moon seemed to hover along with us. My siblings would be squabbling about sharing their toys but I would be in full Starseed flight. Is there really a man in the moon? Could stars shoot out of the sky and send me a wish if I prayed hard enough? Rainbows were extra special with their splendid colours and magical effects. I would imagine beautiful golden buckets, overflowing with magnificent shimmering gold coins, at either end. These are the tools of the Starseed: Imagination and creativity. Were you the child who created a realm of imagination and was quite content in the beauty of the natural world? Starseeds are highly perceptive beings who love nothing more than communing with nature.

Right from my childhood, it was obvious to me that magic, nature and rituals were important signs of a far greater universe than that espoused by organised religion. I would still pray to God – or a higher being – and ask the angels for protection, but my greatest joy came from spending hours in the forest talking to the rocks and flowers and performing elaborate ceremonies. Once I made an offering of fruit and beautiful stones to the higher beings, as I wanted to see my favourite sister-in-law who had just married my eldest brother. Little did I know that I had just carried out my first ever shamanic ritual and, with clear intent, I could not contain my excitement when that very same person arrived that afternoon – just as I had imagined! Did you unwittingly carry out similar rituals as a child and found that, with intention and focus, you could imagine something into your reality? Welcome to the traits of the Starseed child.

"Stop the car!" I screamed, as we travelled up a mountain range on the winding road.

I had been off in my own little world for too long and the momentum of returning to reality had caused the depths of my stomach to erupt into projectile vomiting. Too late. I ejected the foul-smelling contents of my lunch all over myself and the backseat. The vomitus dripped down from my hair all over my favourite holiday clothes. Were you a child overly sensitive to movement shifts, almost as if you are living in several realities at once? This became a familiar occurrence for me along my Starseed journey. I was relegated to the front seat on my mother's lap – no seatbelts or even many road rules back then – thereafter.

Anxiety over changed toilet habits whilst travelling would also often lead me to have an upset stomach with diarrhoea or constipation, or a continual need to pee. This became tortuous for my siblings; we must have stopped at almost every toilet along the way, just in case I needed to go. On one occasion we were almost home to the farm when I could no longer control my need for a bowel movement. We were running out of petrol and Father was worried we would not make it home. He refused to stop so, with one swift move, Mother produced an empty ice-cream bucket. I dropped my pants and expelled the waste. No air-conditioning in those days, so the malodorous smell wafted up from the receptacle to everyone's nostrils. The others began to gag, tears running down their cheeks. To make matters worse there was no toilet paper so newspaper had to suffice. We were about twenty minutes from home when all of them except my parents refused to stay in the car any longer. Father opened the door, and they all piled out and bolted the rest of the way home. Such was my life as an anxious child.

On another occasion we had gone for a day trip to a picnic spot. It was a lovely day but an unwelcome visitor – a green ant – managed to evade detection and slipped unseen onto the back seat. Who should come along and sit on it? You guessed it! The angry ant travelled up my leg to my private parts. Talk about pants on fire! My screams could have woken the dead. Mother stripped me bare to look for the offender. It casually left the scene leaving me with a red raised lump, accompanied by humiliation.

Mosquitoes, bees – in fact any creepy crawly that decided to pierce my skin – would leave me swollen, itchy and sore for days. My fine English rose skin burnt very easily. I would cry for hours as an overreaction to the physical insult, as I felt the uncomfortable sensations too intently.

If you can relate to any of these stories from when you were growing up, then perhaps you are displaying some of the Starseed characteristics: fair, white skin that burns easily, and anxiety over bodily sensations.

This creates a vicious cycle of feeling every emotion from a given event for hours, even days. These emotions were not only mine but also onlookers' and those who created the pain in the first place, including those from the human, plant and animal kingdoms.

Another Starseed characteristic may be an overwhelming fear of water. Many Starseeds on Earth hold the memory of the lost city of Atlantis, the great flood and the falling away of Atlantean existence within their DNA. I have an innate fear of water.

We had many dams on the farm, but we never attempted to go near them as the only member of the family that could swim was our mother; I was terrified of them. My father could not swim; therefore, swimming lessons were not encouraged.

Father had no desire to go holidaying at the beach, but on rare occasions we would spend a week at our grandmother's home at the Gold Coast. Sometimes an extended trip was organised to either Caloundra or Ballina, where we would stay high up on a rocky cliff close to the beach. I loved the feel of the sand on my feet and would spend hours collecting shells, but the waves frightened me and I would only paddle at the sea's edge.

By the end of primary school, I still could not swim efficiently and was banished to the wading pool. The swimming teacher finally decided to end my fear of water forever. Like a prisoner on death row, I was made to plunge into the deep end of the Olympic-sized swimming pool and fight for my existence. The teacher's motto was 'Sink or Swim' and as I sank to the bottom no-one intervened; they hoped that the survival instinct would force me to swim to safety. Fear and panic gripped me – paralysed – as the water held me captive. Finally, I spluttered and flapped around enough to find the edge of the pool. The teacher was not amused and dunked me again. Just as I felt my life ebbing away, I was hauled out of the pool. Cold and shivering, I was marched back to the wading pool to ponder what just happened. I would be forever traumatised by these episodes and have never been able to learn to swim.

It would not be until years later that I would understand the metaphysical reasons behind this fear. Were you a child afraid of water who found it difficult to learn to swim because of a fear you could not explain? Did you have dreams around water or drowning? Perhaps you have a memory of a long-forgotten time – still hidden within your psyche – and related to an ancient lineage that lived in Atlantean times.

Starseeds are exceedingly sentient beings and navigate their way on the earthly plane via their highly tuned thoughts, feelings and emotions. Smells, textures, colours and shapes form an important part of the perception and character of the Starseed generations. For example, to a Starseed, an apple is just not something you eat. Mindfulness is practised so the colour, texture, smell and taste – as well as the environment – is all taken into account before consuming the item. It is, therefore, an experience rather than just an act of culinary delight. Embracing a delicious, juicy, ample apple, rich in colour, under a beautiful tree surrounded by nature, is far more enriching to a Starseed than a store-acquired refrigerated version that lacks flavour and texture. By savouring every morsel and contemplating the feel and texture of the apple in the mouth, the experience takes on a more sacred reverence and a greater sense of gratitude, and happiness transpires.

Christmas and Easter celebrations and shopping expeditions in town were the most magical moments for a Starseed child. I created the most amazing experiences for myself through sheer gratitude and joy. Although not of any particular religious faith, we still engaged in the festivities of Easter egg hunts and hot cross buns, and all the trimmings of a traditional Christmas dinner. The Easter Bunny would leave the most beautiful decorated candy eggs which seemed too delicate, elaborate and intricate to break.

The foil-wrapped chocolate variety were smashed and devoured by my siblings, but I much preferred to slowly unravel the sparkling packaging with its glistening array of colours. The smell and taste of their heavenly creamy texture would linger in the mouth and, together with Mother's delicious homemade ice-cream, made for an exceptional sensory experience. I would always give thanks to God, Jesus and the angels for providing such festivities, even though I did not really understand the true nature of their meaning.

Christmas, in particular, held much delight and anticipation. My sisters and brothers would hitch a ride with Father on the back of an old Dodge truck as we looked forward to fetching a fine conifer tree from the neighbouring forest. Unlike the store variety, the smell of its pine needles was intoxicating. We would place its sturdy trunk into a large bucket of sand, wrapped around with brown paper and tinsel. Most of our tree decorations were homemade but, if we could afford it, Mother would purchase some baubles and figurines from the local op shop. I would be mesmerised by their delicacy and sumptuousness – in particular the majestic glittering star that would sit at the top of the tree.

We had few presents but gleefully unwrapped the beautifully decorated items, including Christmas cards that included pictures of a sparkly Father Christmas with his rosy red chubby cheeks and jovial face. I was enthralled by his jolly disposition and dreamt of his journey with the elves and reindeer over the starry night sky from the North Pole. Would he know to come down our chimney and open fireplace to deliver my very own teddy bear? I prayed every night for my request to be granted and described in my mind to Santa what Teddy would look like: A honey-yellow colour with a cute button nose and a velvet ribbon tied around its neck. In return, I promised to go to bed early and leave out an enormous slice of Christmas cake, together with a glass of warm milk for Santa and his helpers and – of course – carrots for the reindeer.

Wow! I could hardly contain myself when, as if by magic, Teddy arrived and captured my heart. I loved that bear to bits as he provided much love and comfort when I was frightened of the dark and 'things that go bump in the night'. Over fifty years later he is still close to my heart as he sits reassuringly on my mantlepiece.

Were Christmas and Easter celebrations extra special for you because Starseed magic was at play? Did you love the sensory input from all the glitter and sparkles and exquisite smells coming from the kitchen? Did Santa and all the other magical creatures commune with you as a child? And did you ever see a fairy, elf, unicorn or goblin? Nature elementals are around us all the time, and it was many decades later as I opened my mind to greater consciousness that I saw a miniature fairy resemblant of Tinkerbell.

Shopping with Mother at the local jumble sales was another opportunity to practise my sentient awareness. Lots of items all – jumbled up together – made for a delightful discovery tour. A treasure trove of textures, colour and ambience awaited as I played dress-ups, matching different patterns and colours to create an exquisite rainbow of fashion. I marvelled in the sensory explosion of particular fabrics as they flowed and caressed my body. Even though the shoes and dresses were all too big for my small frame. I imagined being all grown up and going to parties and dances like those I had seen in the movies. The sensuality of my feminine Starseed goddess was always yearning for expression and, as an adult, an extensive wardrobe of fashionable outfits holds testament to its undiminished presence. Did you love dressing up in big sisters' clothes and enjoy the different textures, shapes and feel on your body? Some Starseeds hold the feminine goddess energy and will express this in the colours, textures and jewellery they choose to wear.

As I matured, I had plenty of opportunities to embrace the natural world and these are examples of how sentience played an important part in my journey to Starseed knowledge. As you read these stories, imagine yourself as a little child taking in these experiences and see if they conjure up long-forgotten memories of how you, too, experienced the world whilst growing up. Did you rely on your inner-most self to navigate the world or were you more linear in your thoughts and actions? A Starseed employs all of the senses to create their environment; not just the doing process, but always guided by feelings and emotions rather than cognitive thought. Relax and imagine you are there with me.

I had found a special place in the enchanted garden that Father had created and played pretend tea-parties. The gorgeous roses and other ornamentals that he had planted attracted many species of birds who would swoop down and devour the stray cake crumbs left on the plate. My favourite was the male blue wren who, with his magnificent display of plumage, would bathe in the nearby birdbath and then fluff up his feathers to settle in the trees to await a passing insect. I would coo and make bird sounds to attract his attention and in return would be rewarded with a splendid chorus of chirping and frolicking dance moves.

With an inquisitive stare he would cock his head, inviting me to make eye contact. After a shower of rain, the sights and smells in the garden ignited my perception as I put on my raincoat and boots to welcome a spectacular rainbow. The freshness of the grass and the glistening dew drops on the flower petals added to my experience. The sound of green tree frogs invigorated my soul, as did the crisp air and the sun glistening on the last of the raindrops, as they evaporated like magic into another time and space.

In autumn, as the green leaves turned to a patchwork of yellow, brown and red, I put on my warmest coat and hat and bounced through the heaps of vibrant hues. As I skipped, I would invite the leaves to dance with me as the wind lifted their crumpled shapes into the air. The sound of my boots scrunching leaves created the perfect accompaniment as I became lost in the rhythmic beat.

Every so often I would catch a random leaf and crumble it in my hand as the powdery remains fostered new beginnings in the earth. On cold winter mornings I would squeal with delight as the backyard turned into a winter wonderland. I would pretend that I was the Ice Queen and this was my palace. Icicles dripped down from every surface: gutters, roofing and even the clothes line. The grass had turned into a white magic carpet, and the trees and ornamentals that once produced fruit and flowers were now cold white statues waiting to be caressed by the kiss of summer to awaken them.

In the spring, as tiny shoots of new growth began to sprout, I would water this delicate new life. I adored the daffodils and jonquils that provided a long-awaited display of colour after the long harsh winter. Father's lovingly planted and community-minded display of spring blossoms blazed gloriously in the neighbouring streets. A sea of pink engulfed the neighbourhood as thoughts of lazy summer days, family holidays, and the romance and inter-connectedness of life filled the air.

On cold winter nights, I would often accompany Father on his late-night jaunts to pick Mother up from her work as a waitress. Dressed in my new chenille dressing gown and matching slippers I would brave the crisp air to snuggle up on the soft red leather seats of our new Holden in anticipation of the treat Mother would procure for me from the dining room. As we drove through the main street of town, I would press my nose up against the foggy window as my favourite toy store beckoned. There in the window was a variety of dolls and stuffed animals that shone as bright as the stars against the backdrop of the streetlights. Illuminated faces peered out from behind the window – a source of childhood wonder.

As I sat in the parked car, my senses would be heightened as I waited in anticipation for Mother to arrive. I would pass the time by drawing pictures of the toys in the shop on the frosty window. Sometimes I would disengage from my fantasy world and ask my father random questions such as, "What causes the ice on the windscreen?" and "Why does my skin taste salty?" to which a precise reply was always forthcoming.

Mother would arrive in her stained lilac uniform, the smell of fish and chips wafting from the fabric. I did not care as I placed my face into her soft bosom and reached up to give her an enormous hug. She would then present me with either a Coconut Rough or a Mint Pattie. Mmm, delicious! With their glorious round shape wrapped in glistening foil I would savour the flavours. As I slowly opened the brightly coloured packaging and inhaled the aroma, I would immerse myself in the delicacies: their textures delighted me and their chocolate-covered exotic tastes slowly melted in my mouth.

Did you enjoy this journey? What past memories did it conjure up for you? Were you able to experience the same tastes, smells and visual delights? Have you realised that you embrace the world with the same emotional perception as I do? Consider writing your own memories of those sensations you felt as a child to reinvigorate the Starseed within.

CHAPTER TWO

Special Qualities of the Starseed

Starseeds who incarnate on this earthly plane bring with them extraordinary abilities of clairsentience (clear feeling), claircognisance (clear thinking), clairvoyance (clear seeing) and clairaudience (clear hearing). These gifts create an intensely sensitive being with a high level of emotional intelligence and discernment. As my empathic nature continued to manifest, I became aware of an experience known as autonomous sensory meridian response (ASMR), or what is called a brain orgasm. This is a term used to describe an amazing and pleasurable sensation that is not sexual in nature but encompasses profound soul integration and knowingness.

My first introduction to this occurrence presented itself in my early school years. Despite my excellent reading abilities, I found the left-brain reasoning of mathematics difficult. A boy in my class, Tom, who sat next to me, offered to assist. There was only one catch: I was to give him a sneak peek of my undies. Such an odd request I thought. Oh well, here goes. I lifted my skirt to reveal the pretty pink lace knickers which Mother bought for my seventh birthday. It was a quick flash but enough to make a besotted Tom comply with the request. Tom was a typical boy who really did not have much time or patience for girls, but he surprised me with his level of empathy and understanding. Then it happened – his softly spoken voice and complete focus on the job created an intense sensation. It began at the crown chakra and slowly moved down the neck, into the spine and across the shoulders. I was overcome with the beautiful feeling which came in intense waves. I was in a state of bliss until a strong poke in the ribs for not answering his question brought me back to the reality of Tom and the mathematical equations.

I had many other experiences of ASMR and began to think that it was a natural part of being human. I found that they were random events and simply could not be conjured into creation, unlike the plethora of videos available today that provide an artificial environment for the stimuli to occur. Specific words, tones, or touching something that is connected to me, were triggers for the sensation. They were not associated with any particular gender, age, race or culture. I do not have to particularly like the person providing the exchange, but the intensity is even more evident if that person is usually cold and lacking empathy. It is as if one penetrates the mask behind the uncaring attitude.

I have often wondered if the process is reciprocal and if the other party feels the same vibes. I have come to the conclusion that some more enlightened beings will be aware of the sense of oneness, but some fifty years after my first experience, I have not had anyone whisper in my ear and say, "Did the earth move for you too?"! What a wonderful world it would be if all of us – through random acts of kindness – experienced this universal gift on a regular basis. There would be no wars, no time for hate and ignorance.

Has this ever happened to you? Did you talk to others about it and found that you could not find anyone who understood what you had experienced? Write examples here of when, where, how and why it happened, and the impact it had on your level of love and compassion for others. Does it happen randomly or can you make it happen at will?

When I was in my early twenties, my interest in alternative medicine led to the attainment of naturopathic qualifications. It was combined with a deep interest and desire for knowledge in the world of Spirit. I devoured every book I could find on the subject of 'The New Age Movement', as it was called. I researched near-death experiences (NDEs), astrology, aliens and the afterlife. I read of books from Dawn Hill to Louise Hay and magazines such as Nexus and Wellbeing. I also began meditating on a regular basis.

Do you have an interest in spiritual matters and do you meditate regularly? Are you aware of spirits or angels around you? Have you ever wondered if guardian angels are watching over you and trying to communicate with you?

The Starseed journey begins with the ability to meditate and open up to the other realms. As my mind continued to expand and appreciate long-hidden abilities, I encountered my first episode of sleep paralysis. This frightening sensation occurs between wakefulness and sleep causing a person to become completely paralysed. Some cultures believe it is a pesky ghost or demon who has become earthbound and seeks to reside in another body, or who cannot find the light to move on to another plane. My experiences with sleep paralysis, however, are more transcendental – my consciousness expanded to be in two places at once.

It was early morning and as I was sleeping, I heard the sound of glass crashing. In the loungeroom was a fish tank, so my consciousness considered the possibility that it had given way and, therefore, water would be all over the floor. Then I heard the sound of cups and saucers rattling, cupboards banging and footsteps, as if someone had broken into the premises and was preparing a meal in the kitchen.

My heart began to race as I thought about this stranger and wondered how I was to escape through the back door without disturbing the intruder. The adrenaline kicked in and as I went to lunge off the bed to escape, I was terrified to discover that my body simply would not move! No matter how much I tried to cajole my inert body into action I was completely paralysed – including my voice which created no sound when I attempted to scream.

I lay there for what seemed like hours. Eventually I noticed that the noise had ceased and, just like a patient recovering from the effects of anaesthetic, my body was coming back to life. When I felt sensation in my limbs, I crept out along the hallway and peered around the corner in the direction of the fish tank. To my amazement it was still standing, proudly displaying the magnificent goldfish I had recently purchased.

There was no sign of a forced entry so I thought perhaps it was an old boyfriend coming to collect some gear and who had stopped to have a coffee. The kitchen was just as I had left it the night before. All the dishes were neatly stacked away and there was no sign of open cupboards, or that anyone had prepared a meal. All other rooms were empty and nothing had been stolen. Perplexed, I later contacted old flatmates to see if they still had keys to the premises but they had all been handed back.

Then I began to question whether my bizarre paralysis state was an out-of-body experience and that it was, in fact, me – in spiritual form – in the kitchen. It still did not make a whole lot of sense and not until years later when I discovered the concept of parallel realities and timelines.

Have you had such an experience that you could not quite fathom? Did you believe there were entities pinning you down or do you believe you left your body and travelled elsewhere? It can be frightening, can it not? Many Starseed species are proficient at out-of-body experiences and encountering entities from both the dark and the light. Starseeds are highly skilled in telepathy, so you may find yourself talking with entities via the mind.

Many years ago, I received a premonition in the form of an apparition which appeared before me whilst I slept. I was transfixed by its luminous form, and began to receive a telepathic message that my parents were not well. With no landline, I waited until the morning and hurried to the local phone box to call. My mother answered, and as I asked if all was well, she replied that Father had run into the wall in the night, had broken a rib and that she was feeling poorly and would see the doctor.

For some time, I had felt an uneasiness concerning my mother's health. I had taken an overseas trip and as she helped me pack, I could not shake the feeling that something was not quite right. It turned out she had advanced cancer and had only nine months to live.

Have you received telepathic messages from the spirit world? Do you trust your gut instinct? Are you frightened by these messages or do you find them comforting?

I have been immensely comforted by the visitations from loved ones who have passed. One night, whilst sleeping, I was roused by a sensation that someone was sitting on the side of my bed watching over me. As I became conscious of my surroundings, I cried out, "Who is there – what do you want?" Then, struggling to wake, I felt a presence lift the blanket from the bottom of the bed and gently place it over my body up to my shoulders – like a mother's action ensuring her child was warm and cosy. I opened my eyes and felt it disappear as I lay wondering if I had imagined the whole episode. On reflection, I thought about this visitation, and, as I sat in prayerful meditation, was intuitively given a name. It was a woman who had recently died; she had been like a second mother to me. I understood that she was taking advantage of my ability to communicate beyond the veil and to reassure me that all was well.

As I watched Mother take her final breath, my heart contorted as I cried out in grief. I felt a gentle tugging at my solar plexus as if the umbilical cord of our connection in this lifetime was being cut. As I sat beside her now still body I could not help notice how in death her physicality stood out.

It was evident that her spiritual essence – the part that lit up her face and animated her eyes – had now gone leaving only the outer shell to take centre stage. In her final days I asked Mother to give me a sign as evidence of her newfound spiritual existence and it was not long before she answered my request.

Whilst having a nap, my olfactory sense was aroused by a sweet-smelling aroma wafting up my nostrils. It persisted, becoming more pronounced, and my brain registered its familiarity as I yelled out, "Mamma! Is that you?" It seems my mother communicated in the only way she knew how. For Mother there was never a signature perfume to remember her by. Sadly, the sickly-sweet odour of a cancerous death was the indelible effect left on the family psyche.

I sat bolt upright in bed, frantically looking for a glimpse of a ghostly apparition or any movement of objects. Alas, my clairvoyance was not apparent. Thankfully, my clairsentient ability was now well-established as I felt her loving presence. This would be how we would communicate for many years to come, with Mother often visiting when I was alone or sad. My two sisters and my father also had the same visitations.

My father had a scientific explanation for everything; therefore, he was dumbfounded when, every time he gave me a hug, I could smell her presence on his clothing. Mother visited one sister on a suburban train and the other had experiences of lights turning on and off, and 'that smell' wafting out of the cupboards and all through the house.

Mamma had long ended her visitations once Father had entered the afterlife and I missed the comfort of their loving presence. One night I was stirred from my sleep by the silhouette of a man sitting on the edge of my bed.

"Father!" I cried out in my mind.

"Yes Kid," (he always called me 'Kid') "it is me."

Through telepathy we spoke to each other's minds. I could see him in my mind's eye, but he was now a much younger version of himself: Such a handsome man with dark hair and, of course, his beautiful cornflower-blue eyes. He looked relaxed and happy, but was definitely here for a reason. Tears rolled down my cheeks as he expressed his deep regret at some bad karma that had existed between us prior to his death. I could feel his infinite love touch me and instantly I felt comforted and safe. I wanted to know more about his journey since leaving Earth and as I came out of my trance state, reached to embrace him but he was gone…

It was like all of the hurt feelings between us had never existed and, for the first time since his passing, I felt free of regret, guilt and pain. I now knew that I was always loved, and would continue to be loved, even if we were no longer together physically.

Have you had such experiences with departed loved ones through communication via extra-sensory abilities? Did you find a sense of peace and comfort from their presence? Perhaps you have been visited by a beloved deceased pet or have had them communicate in such a way as to know that they are happy and safe in another realm. Starseeds have no problem communicating with the dead and their highly tuned resonance acts like a decoder of messages from beyond the grave.

This encounter taught me a valuable lesson. It does not matter who you are, what you have done, or how wealthy or entitled you felt in the physical world, when you die the only thing that matters are the memories and the love we gave. No-one will remember us for the way we looked, or the possessions we had, but they will remember how kind and inspiring we were.

Have you had regrets about things unsaid or feelings not demonstrated prior to a loved one's departure? Have you had a visitation that changed your whole perspective on the afterlife and how to live your best life? Write your thoughts about those who may have wronged you whilst here on Earth. Can you forgive and show compassion for those who may have harmed you? Equally, can you feel the same about yourself if you wronged someone who is now departed?

Starseeds see the beauty in the all: There is no good or bad, just experiences as part of the evolution of the soul.

My Starseed abilities also provide me with a close connection to electricity and water. In 1980 I purchased a waterbed – all the rage at the time. It was not long before I realised that, if someone was to sit on the bed with me and I touched them, the sensation would be like that of a vibrator on their skin. I also learned that I could transfer this experience to others in the shower, in an electrical storm, or touching wet hair whilst using a hairdryer. My father was a water diviner so perhaps I inherited this ability from him. Whatever the reason, it would freak out those who experienced the occurrence. As my girlfriend, Nancy, and I sat on the edge of the waterbed talking, I leaned over to touch her arm. The vibrations appeared on cue. Unperturbed, at first, by this strange happening, I demonstrated the energy field by moving my hands further down her arm. Nancy stopped talking and said she was feeling cold.

"Can you smell that strange odour?" she asked.

"What does it smell like?"

"Very sweet and pungent," she said.

Before I had a chance to answer, she yelled, "Stop with the vibrating – Mother is here."

Nancy had no prior knowledge of Mother's interesting calling card or her Saturday night visits, so I was surprised by her revelation. This time I could not detect any odour: it was purely a message for Nancy. For her, however, it was all too much and she leapt off the bed and left the room.

Have you had similar experiences with water and electricity? Are you able to shower in an electrical storm without getting surges of electricity through your feet? Are other electrical appliances – such as lights and mobile phones – affected by your resonance? I cannot tolerate mobile phones anywhere near the vicinity of my auditory canal, otherwise I receive all sorts of beeping noises, including something that sounds similar to Morse code.

Some Starseeds have innate healing abilities, manifested by simply touching a person, or through a kind word or gesture. Others' amazing abilities include remote or distance healing.

The Universe was beckoning me to explore other healing modalities so I joined a meditation class and met like-minded individuals. John was the leader of the class and it was not long before I was experiencing interesting phenomenon whilst participating in hands-on healing. As I placed my hands about six inches away from my female nominated volunteer I abruptly moved into a trance-like state. With my eyes closed, I felt my hands grasp her head and rotate it clockwise vigorously. The poor woman's head had become like the agitator in a washing machine as it swirled back and forth.

Aghast, and out of the trance, I peeked with one eye to see how she was reacting. I found her head was as still as a tranquil lake, with my hands six inches from her skull. I could not believe what I had just witnessed and neither could the woman, when she asked me what I had experienced. To my amazement, she had felt every movement I had initiated and thought I had grabbed her head and reefed it from side to side. John was ecstatic with my innate ability and suggested that I should further nurture this gift. As I continued to meditate, I regularly sensed pulsing and burning in my hands which enhanced my skills in massage and other bodywork.

I decided to attend a course with my naturopath colleague, Kristen, so I could extend my knowledge of vibrational or energy medicine. The course was called Body Electronics and, as the name suggests, the hands-on techniques were designed to lift the vibrational status of the body by removing blocks in energy centres – chakras – through sustained point-holding. The technique was originally developed by Dr John Whitman Ray. Removing mental and emotional blocks holding us back from knowing our spiritual self was an arduous and painstaking journey. I witnessed physical gyrations and emotional release like never before and decided to embrace whatever came up for me.

As Kristen sustained pressure on my upper back, a world of emotional pain came exploding through my body as it writhed and vibrated in anguish. All the past hurts: Being mistreated by childhood teachers were exposed, the pungent smell of anaesthetic from the myriad operations I had endured, and pesticides held deep within the tissues. The smell wafted through the room, making the attendees violently ill and wanting to vomit. This release went on for hours as, once locked into points on the body, the finger points could not be disconnected from the electrical grid until there was no more burning coming through.

Preparation for these sessions took days of consuming colloidal minerals, a clean diet and supplements, in order to obtain the charge required to connect to the body. It was all rather barbaric and by the end of the day I was feeling exhausted. I was staying at Kristen's place and she decided to go and get take-away dinner without me whilst I had a rest.

Once alone, I relaxed on the bed only to experience the most excruciating sudden crushing pain in my chest, ribs and upper back. I tried to stay calm as I gasped and wondered if I was having a heart attack. What happened next had a profound effect: As I breathed to control the pain, I was shocked to find my right-hand upper ribcage extend dramatically outwards. Before, this part of my ribcage was contracted and curved inward due to scoliosis as a result of rickets.

I watched in awe as it gyrated to become a perfect match to the corresponding left ribcage. I could not express my amazement, and when Kirsten arrived home, she too was speechless when I showed her my newfound body structure. I was gobsmacked, being familiar with my nude body – in all its glory – I was well aware of my stunted ribcage and the spinal curvature affecting my upper back.

I continued to have those extraordinary occurrences through the next few years, including an episode of what I now know as 'light language'. I sat bolt upright in bed one night, still asleep. and proceeded to give a very measured speech in what was thought to be Latin. Then I lay back down and, much to my husband's disappointment, had no recollection of it the next day. He was determined to make a recording next time. Unfortunately, it did not happen again for well over twenty years.

Have you always had an interest in healing modalities, particularly those that pertain to energy or vibrational medicine? Have you attended courses where something unusual has happened to you or others around you? Have you ever spoken in a language that others could not comprehend? Write your experiences here.

Starseeds can easily access the higher dimensions and can alter time-space reality at will. My first experience with alternate realities came in 2006. Whilst travelling after work, I came upon an idiot in a ute who was attempting a burnout, lost control and was careering head-on in my direction. I had nowhere to go to avoid the collision, so I surrendered to whatever was to occur.

At that second, I heard the crash of steel on steel. Eyes shut, I prepared for unknown injuries. I came to a halt. The guy in the ute got out of his vehicle and walked towards me.

"Are you alright?" he asked.

"Yes, I think so," I said, startled, "but I am not sure about my car."

He looked perplexed and suggested I start the engine, and pull over onto a side road. He would take a look.

I was relieved to find the motor responded immediately. I crept slowly off the main road. In the meantime, the guy 'pulled a swifty' and left the scene – no name, no phone number or licence details. That'd be right! I fumed as I got up enough courage to inspect the damage. I stepped out of the car and peeked around to the front of the vehicle. I could not believe the sight before me. Not so much as a scratch, let alone a dint, could be found and yet I distinctly heard the sound of an almighty smash.

I stood there for what seemed like forever before I finally came out of my daze. I continued on my journey, but later on that evening burst into tears with delayed shock. Whatever miracle had been bestowed on me that day awoke me again to the wonders of unseen worlds.

Many years later I came to realise that I had been powerful enough to manipulate time and space, and to switch my reality into another dimension, thus saving myself and my car from what had appeared to be an inevitable fate. No wonder the guy took off and gave me such a perplexed look! He is probably still trying to figure out how the hell his ute was undamaged, let alone how my car could be in one piece since he had been responsible for the 'almost accident'.

Have you experienced an episode of alternate realities – as if you are living in two places at once? Have you a story such as mine where you have miraculously changed a situation to avoid either death or injury?

How did you feel afterwards? Why was it such a powerful experience and how did it change your perspective on your own reality?

Some Starseeds are prophetic dreamers and as past, present and future are all happening at once in the world of quantum reality, they can access valuable information via lucid dreaming. This happens when you are actively involved in the dream as if it is a part of your reality. You remember every detail of the situation compared to regular dreaming where you simply forget it the next day.

Prior to having a prophetic dream in 2010, I witnessed a bizarre gyration on my abdomen. How to explain this? Rolls of wave-like muscle movements commenced at my lower abdomen undulating to my upper torso. I watched in disbelief as I saw my tummy convulsing in a way enough to make any belly dancer proud; however, the movements were not of my making – I had no control over their dance.

Six months later whilst lucid dreaming at a beautiful home I once owned, I found myself walking the surrounding roads only to find there were no houses, only empty blocks of land. In the dream I searched and searched for people, but there were none to be found. Thinking it may have been a premonition for a fire, I put the dream to the back of my mind until a gigantic weather event disclosed the reason for the warning.

Two weeks prior to 10th January, 2011, my anxiety went through the roof. Was something of a catastrophic nature about to happen? I could not sleep and paced the house most of the night, and trembled uncontrollably during the day. Waves of impending doom hit me from every direction.

I hugged my daughter tight as I waited for the sign. It had been raining all week and the rivers and creeks were overflowing. The children were on school break and we were at home listening to the deluge, when a heavy lightning bolt hit the roof. Mother Nature unleashed her fury on an unsuspecting community.

Unable to hear anything except the thunderous sound of torrents of water, I looked out the window to see streams of water covering the roads as the stormwater drains backed up. I felt the familiar sense of apprehension as I noticed the water beginning to rise in the backyard. It was not long before it was lapping at the door and then, within an instant, entered the premises. Frantically, we struggled to move our belongings higher as it began to swirl like a slippery snake, finding any entrance it could. Out came the shovel, and I frantically dug a new pathway to allow the menacing water to escape, whilst seven-year-old Cheri took charge inside. The rain did not last for long, but in its wake, it left its mark of destruction and devastation.

A 'wall of water' – an inland tsunami – destroyed the area, with cars and property upended and houses destroyed. Tragically, lives were lost and, shockingly, in an area I had once lived. Sadness and despair would affect people for many years but, paradoxically, community awareness and togetherness became of paramount importance during this difficult time.

It was not until a few years later that I realised the prophetic dream I had experienced was a precursor of the weather event, and my own experiences with water and electricity had heightened the messages coming through from Mother Earth.

In my dream, where I walked from property to property and found no houses, I had thought I had witnessed a catastrophic bushfire. It was now clear that the houses had not burnt down, but been washed away by an extraordinary flood. The rolling waves I had felt on my physical body were the manifestation of the storm's fallout.

Have you had prophetic dreams? Do you experience extreme bodily sensations that warn you of impending disaster? What type of symptoms do you experience?

_____

_____

_____

_____

_____

_____

CHAPTER THREE

The Dark Night of the Soul – the Awakening Begins

One Starseed trait which stands out from other gifted humans is the constant feeling of 'wanting to go home'. Not just a feeling of being different, or the black sheep of the family because you act and think differently, but the relentless 'homesickness' for some other existence. This is a different concept to past lives – of having previously reincarnated on this earth – but it is a deep and heartfelt feeling that your roots are not of this earthly realm. If this answer resonates with you, then read on as I begin my journey into realising something quite extraordinary and profound. I am indeed connected to other unworldly beings that extend far beyond this existence of time and space.

It began with a seemingly innocent trip to the supermarket. As I began filling my basket with essential items, I felt a bizarre sensation of not really being in the here and now. My head began to spin as a powerful energy caused me to lunge forward as I grabbled to keep my balance. I was terrified as I lost control of my sense of spatial awareness. I began to shake uncontrollably, dropped the basket, and held onto the walls and then the stairs, until I made it to the car. Feeling nauseous, and with a racing heart, I somehow managed to make it home. After resting, I returned to equilibrium, but it was not long before the sensation happened again.

This disequilibrium became my new norm as I struggled to negotiate everyday life. I had also become increasingly photophobic and could not tolerate natural sunlight without darkened glasses. Fluorescent lighting, flashing lights of any kind, and even loud noise would send my body into a state of unbalance. The powerful force of the sun created a magnetic pull which created such a surge of anxiety that often times I wanted to flee from its presence. Driving a car became a restrictive nightmare. I only drove at night in the dark. Strangely, the cars' headlights had no effect, and the moonlight – rather than create an anguished state – made me feel calm and in control.

I noticed that complex patterning on clothing – such as leopard print or geometric shapes – would appear to shimmer, as did looking at photographs in glass frames. Also disturbing, was the pulsating occurrence which seemed to pass through my eyes as I stared into the distance, and the continuing river of pulses that emanated from my hands.

I still tried to see patients from home but I was too ill to work, as every ounce of energy seemed to be draining from my body. I had lost a considerable amount of weight and my clothes became loose and ill-fitting. I had no appetite and felt like a ragdoll as I tried to feed and dress myself with trembling hands. I looked in the mirror and swore I had aged dramatically. My face was wrinkled and took on a sunken appearance and my hair was thin and sparse. As my eyes stared back from the mirror, I could not recognise myself: It was as if I was no longer me. I seemed to have taken on a mesmerised appearance, as if possessed by the Madhatter. Even my little dog was scared of this stranger, somehow sensing that the person I had been had disappeared.

After myriad of X-rays, blood tests and scans revealed no obvious abnormalities, it was suggested that my condition was purely psychological and that I needed to be on an antidepressant. As a naturopath, the thought horrified me. I began a series of detoxes, hormone- and gut-balancing, and adrenal support to get myself back on track. I had fallen foul of the medical profession in my youth and I tried to find a natural approach to this puzzling condition. I visited various practitioners, including bodywork and energy remedies, but nothing would shift the feeling of disassociation and impending doom. It sat in my gut and refused to abate. The intense anxiety made me feel I was about to die, as surges of tingling and cold sensations ran up and down my spine. I screamed as the world spun. Nauseous, and regurgitating my saliva, I cried out to the Universe to take this monster away.

After a week on pharmaceutical medication, death felt it would be a blessing as my body violently rejected this chemical assault. Abdominal cramps and diarrhoea had me writhing in pain and I became even more psychotic as I crouched in a cupboard shaking uncontrollably, barely able to speak. It was decided, as the drugs were causing serotonin syndrome*, I would have no choice but to take an alternative: Benzodiazepine or Valium. Now I could function without the awful anxiety; my intruder from hell. The downside was that this medication is highly addictive, so I was forced to use it sparingly. Without it, I could not drive my daughter to school since stopping at intersections became my new nightmare.

Travelling in the car was fine until I came to a standstill at traffic lights. Then the cars on either side of me seemed as if they were still moving and, even though I had my foot on the brake, I too felt like I was either moving backwards if on a slope, or still moving forwards; the illusion of movement. The sun blazing down on the windscreen would exacerbate the situation as I felt my spiritual self try to lift out of my physical body to escape the light.

Insomnia also became a companion as I tried to get a good night's sleep. As soon as I snuggled under the covers of a warm, welcoming bed and began to fall asleep, I would be woken by violent muscle jerking. Myoclonus, they call it. It is unconscious: Uncontrollable muscle spasms cause limbs to gyrate and contort. My head would thrust about wildly. The more I tried to open the gate to nocturnal oblivion, the worse the situation became, so I would surrender and spend most of the night awake until my body finally had no choice but to enter the twilight zone. If I woke again, however, the process would resume.

*https://en.wikipedia.org/wiki/Serotonin_syndrome

When I was not having uncontrollable muscle spasms, I would hear clicking noises in my mouth and head, along with the incessant sound of ringing in the ears. Sometimes I felt like I was being touched on the face, and the most disturbing of all were the strange tones that sounded as if someone was changing the frequency on a radio dial, except it was coming from my ear! Other auditory illusions – such as hearing easy-listening music or a choir of angels singing – would soon follow.

I went for auditory testing and it was found that I had the hearing of a twenty-year-old in one ear – for which there was no explanation. Visits to neurologists and ear specialists followed with no elucidation for my bizarre symptoms other than to suggest anxiety. In fact, one arrogant ear specialist suggested that I should combine my Valium with alcohol and I would no longer have any anxiety! I began to doubt my sanity until something huge happened that changed my perspective. Between the disabling effects of dizziness and depression I would have bouts of extreme flu-like symptoms. Pathology tests confirmed that I was perfectly healthy, even though I felt like a rag doll and could barely lift my arms to dress myself.

I gave up on pharmaceutical medications and sought counsel from my spiritual friend. His revelation opened the door to a new understanding.

"It seems you are suffering from Ascension Flu," he said.

"What is that?"

"Your energy body is changing to a higher frequency, otherwise known as The Awakening. You are raising your consciousness to a higher level and removing all the old energy blocks that have been holding you back. That is why you are suffering so many bizarre symptoms, because your body is burning off the dross of so many lifetimes and ancestral patterning." He looked at me with his wise blue eyes. "In other words, you have blown a fuse in your nervous system."

"Whaat? How do I fix it?"

"You don't," he replied. "Just Be. Allow the Universe to unfold within. Your DNA is getting an upgrade as the spiritual veil is lifted and you become more conscious of other realms and dimensions. Rest and meditate, and if the process becomes too much, ask the angels and higher beings to help you on the journey."

I had not meditated seriously for quite some time; I had been caught up in the frenetic pace of life and motherhood. Unable to work full-time, I allowed my body to relax into a meditative space. I began to sense soft feather-like caresses on my face and crown, reassuring me all was well. For the first time in so long I felt less alone – and at peace. I incorporated meditation into my life each day and decided to add in a few other divination tools, such as tarot cards and a pendulum. I went back to reading spiritual books, something I had abandoned years before, but in particular those on ascension and The Awakening. It was all starting to make much more sense, even though I still struggled every day with balance and dizziness.

As I spent more and more time in an introspective state away from the outside world, I began to tune more effectively to the rhythm of Mother Earth. I knew I would know in advance if any environmental disaster was about to befall on the planet. Earthquakes and tidal waves leading to tsunami disasters in particular, had me pacing for hours prior to the event.

My interest in numerology also led me to notice a pattern in the numbers associated with the dates of events. An interesting coincidence was that the dates of these disasters added up to the number 11. At least two had the number 11 in the date (11:11) or two of the number 22 (22:22). I started to home in on the fascinating connection with the number 11. It was everywhere! Both these numbers are called 'master numbers' in numerology and I began to wonder if they had played a significant part in my life so far. I realised I held the master number 11 in my numerology chart, and that this number was a highly significant number for the awakening process.

As I looked back on my life and the events that happened to me every 11 years, I became ever more intrigued. At the age of 11 I had bone issues; at 22 I had 'come of age'; at 33 I got engaged; at 44 I lost my home and business, and at 55 suffered from physical disability once again. I further broke these number sequences into significant years adding up to 11: at

29 years I met my husband and lost my own mother; at 38 I became a mother myself, at 47 I went through the change of life and at 56 became menopausal and ceased the physical ability to create life.

With this reignited interest in numerology, I began to experience lucid dreams and had difficulty falling and staying asleep. When I looked for the time, the numbers would always add up to that curious number 11. My body would jerk uncontrollably and in meditation my body would contort into weird positions called Kriyas, with unconscious hand movements called mudras*.

Whilst holding my crystals I would tune into their resonance and my hands would pulse in synchronicity. I would often be woken up by the sound of beautiful music, like a harp, or sometimes easy-listening guitar music. Sometimes in the shower my ears would resonate with the water, the copper pipes creating tones; and at other times I could distinctly hear a low humming coming from the Earth.

My ears perceived various tones – beeping, clicking, buzzing, whooshing and ringing – and would resonate with the electrical appliances inside the home, as well as overhead telephone lines. Through lack of sleep, and the strange resonance in my head, I would often wake with blurred vision – it would last for hours. At other times small bright purple sparkles came and went randomly, along with a feeling of pulsing in my vision.

I thought there was something wrong with my eyes, so I decided to have a thorough examination with an eminent eye clinic, only to be told that there was nothing physically wrong. I was relieved but was left curious about an additional comment, "You have very fine energy resonance which is why you feel the pulsing sensation."

Despite being cleared of anything sinister, I decided to get the opinion of another ear specialist. This person found a vestibular weakness, probably as a result of exposure to human parvovirus I had contracted the previous year. It was also suggested I had developed vestibular migraine. This condition may not cause a headache, but can result in symptoms such as photosensitivity and disequilibrium. With no known cure, it is

*Kriya and mudra are Sanskrit words.

debilitating. There is often a history of migraines and, on reflection, I had suffered aura without headache during pregnancy. Previous concussions, or neck and head injuries, have also been implicated in their occurrence, and I have certainly had plenty of those.

I felt such relief that my symptoms had a physical cause. It was then that I decided to dismiss the advice from my meditation teacher that this was purely a spiritual ascension process. I gave up meditating and concentrated on vestibular rehabilitation and cognitive behavioural therapy to cope with the condition.

How wrong was I to embrace the physical and psychological aspects but completely ignore the spiritual aspects? It was time to wake up! The more I ignored the issue, the more the Universe persisted in delivering increasingly hard-to-ignore signs. The lucid dreams began in earnest, as well as the number 11 appearing constantly on my mobile phone.

One day, as I was leaving to go out, I noticed an object on the driveway. Unable to reverse the car without moving it, I had a closer look. I found an old garden ornament – a duck – lying on its side. It was antiquated, it looked as if it was a relic from the past. Obviously, somebody did not appreciate its appearance and, as I was about to place it in the rubbish bin, I felt compassion for this inanimate object. I grabbed the hose, gave it a quick clean and left it on the porch to dry. Little did I realise that by touching and accepting the energy exchange, my life would become truly woo-woo!

When I got home, I noticed it had shifted slightly. I thought the wind must have moved it, so I put it back where I had left it and went inside. The next day the duck had disappeared. I thought it must have been taken by a marauding cat or dog, so imagine my surprise, when I went out into the backyard to retrieve some washing, where I found it lying on its side.

How bizarre, I thought. I wondered why anybody would go to such extremes: Pick it up off the porch and throw it into the backyard. You would have to walk around the back of the property, as there was no access gate. I decided to leave it inside the house and, did not think any more about it.

The next morning, I went outside to collect the mail and noticed my fully-opened umbrella on the porch. What is this doing here? I took it back inside. There had been no rain the previous week and I wondered if I had somehow misplaced it down the road and someone had returned it. What a curiosity! Then my rational brain thought perhaps it had rained and I had just forgotten I used it and had left it out to dry. I put it down to forgetfulness and placed the umbrella back in the cupboard. The little duck caught my eye, sitting there on the side table. I decided to give it a wash and, as the warm soap suds removed the dust and grime, I noticed its dark beady eyes penetrating mine as if they were somehow alive. Again I considered throwing it away, but as I had gone to so much trouble to give it a makeover, decided to put it back on the porch.

Each day I would find the little duck had moved. Sometimes it would have moved slightly to the left, and other times to the right, and other times it would flip back onto its side. Had the wind been blowing and moved it into another position? No, most days had been calm with only a slight breeze.

The beady-eyed duck

I am someone who pays a lot of attention to detail and I noticed other little things happening inside the house. Ornaments would be moved slightly out of place, or disappear altogether. In particular, there was a photo of me that, every morning, would be face down on the floor in the loungeroom. I no longer had my pussycats to blame, and my little dog was not agile enough to jump up to such a height and knock things over.

I was now a little disturbed by these happenings and I told my friends at a clinic where I worked. I was jokingly told, "You probably took the ghost home with you!"

"What ghost?" I asked, astonished.

Apparently, a resident ghost at the work premises often moves items about in the clinic, and doors often open and close by themselves. The staff seemed to think the ghost is female, as people have heard a woman's voice crying for help when there is no-one else around. The staff had used incense to try and get the ghost to move on. Had it hitched a ride with me? I decided to use sage incense throughout the house to see if that made a difference, but the movements continued.

It was at this time that the first of a number of disturbing events happened. My daughter had taken a shower and came out to ask me about something she had seen in the mirror.

"Did you put that there?" she asked.

I gazed up at the very top of the mirror and I was shocked to see the shape of two very large hands.

I could not believe the vision before me and my mind raced for a logical answer. Neither of us have hands anywhere near that big, so we concluded that they definitely belonged to a male. My husband had taken a nursing contract and would be gone for several months and his hands were nowhere near as huge. My heart froze. Was an intruder hiding in the house? Was that the reason why items had been disturbed?

I stared in consternation as the hands had not only left an imprint, but all the lines on the palms could be seen clearly. It almost looked like someone was behind the mirror and had placed their hands on the glass. Such detail! This image was as lifelike as a photograph, so I took a camera shot for evidence.

After a few days of no further occurrences, the hands were starting to give me the creeps, so I decided to rub them off. The imprint was removed easily and, relieved, I was less troubled. About a week later I had the front door open; it is in direct line of sight to the bathroom mirror. I was watering the garden when I looked across in the direction of the bathroom. There were the hands on the mirror again. I dropped the hose in disbelief. I hurried inside and, yep, it was exactly the same detail, but placed lower down on the mirror surface. I had the strangest feeling that the hands only appeared once I opened the front door and, ridiculously, that it had something to do with the little duck with its beady black eyes.

Large human-like hands on the mirror

As the weeks passed, hands began to appear elsewhere in the house, and a whole row of them merged together on the sliding glass door into the garden. It was not long before they appeared in my daughter's room, but this time they were more like an outline of a hand, and some appeared in a creepy skeletal form.

Creepy skeletal apparition of a hand on the wall

The skeletal-type fingers were long and tapered; giving them a vaguely demonic appearance. Over time, all the walls began to display an array of hands of various shapes and sizes. They were reminiscent of those found in ancient caves throughout the world. Some of the imprints were arranged in a circular shape as if representing some sort of vortex or portal. It reminded me of the shape of the UNICEF symbol, but instead of olive branches, they looked like children's hands. Most intriguing, however, were the symbols that appeared on the ceiling of the bedroom. They looked like someone had been drawing in dust; except these could not be rubbed off. It was as if they had been imprinted into the paintwork.

I researched their meaning and was intrigued to find that these particular markings have been found in ancient caves around the globe. It is as if they try to tell a story in an ancient language and the symbols are represented by what are described as finger flutes, penniforms*, crosshatches and fan-shaped hands. I had never seen these images before, and neither had my daughter who was becoming increasingly uneasy sleeping in her bedroom.

*A symbol shaped like a feather.

It was not long before the hands appeared in other parts of the house. There were also strange flecks of light – like shiny bright stars – that also appeared within the portal of hands, and a shimmer of bright flecking appeared on the kitchen ceiling. It was as if the night sky, in all its splendour, was being reflected back to me.

A different type of marking appeared in my clinic room. Odd-looking shapes arranged in a square stared back at me from the ceiling. I thought they were water marks, so the roof was inspected for leakage. There was no leak, neither had there been any recent rain, and these marks – together with the others – had appeared virtually overnight.

My rational mind was still considering that perhaps someone was entering the premises whilst we were away and playing a sick joke. But another part of me felt strangely comfortable with the situation. I reasoned that maybe the paintwork was deteriorating and leaving these strange images, but this idea was shattered. Further activity broke down what I considered my reality.

Markings left on the bedroom ceiling

CHAPTER FOUR

The Illusion of Reality – the Dragon, the Lion and the Shaman

Now I really was starting to feel a little frightened and beginning to think that this was not human intervention, but paranormal activity.

I decided to seek the services of a psychic who cleanses houses. An appointment was made for her to visit the property, but at the last minute she could not make it; several further attempts always presented an issue and she did not show up. It was almost as if 'whatever it was' did not want her interference. I gave up on that idea. I also showed the photo to a clairvoyant to see if she thought it was a malevolent being. She could not give me an explanation but suggested that it was an Indigenous man and that the knocking over of ornaments was my own deceased cats in spirit form.

One night my daughter woke up screaming that a man with long hair had come out of the ceiling and stared at her from above. When she turned on the light there, at the top of her bedhead, was a large skeletal handprint on the wall. As well, she had just obtained her driver's licence and been gifted a car by her auntie. Overnight, hand marks appeared all over the car in the familiar style and shape. Another interesting phenomenon were scratches, like claw marks, left on the windscreen and on the bedroom doors. Each time I hosed the marks off the car, a peculiar musty earthy smell would waft into the air as if something had been unleashed from the earth below. No matter how hard I scrubbed the marks could not be removed. It was as if they had been sand-blasted into the glass.

I was uneasy and became concerned about her driving the car. It was not long before my concerns eventuated when, one night coming home from work, she was involved in an accident. Luckily, she was unhurt but the car was nearly a write-off. Understandably, she was no longer comfortable driving so, after some repairs, I began to use the car to drive her to work.

One day, as I went to wash off the creepy hand marks again, I noticed there was something underneath the car. I reversed it out of the way to take a closer look and there were two huge gleaming pieces of obsidian*. What the hell? How in the world did these get here? I picked them up and stared intently at their awesomeness. I could not fathom how anyone in their right mind would place them there, let alone give them away, as they would have been worth a few dollars.

I was about to claim them for myself when fear gripped my stomach and a voice inside whispered, Remember what happened the last time you picked something off the road. Fear overrode me and I threw the precious rocks as hard as I could onto the road and scurried back inside. I had convinced myself the items were cursed and that somehow that duck was the cause of it all. I now set about ridding myself of that duck permanently.

The duck's black beady eyes stared ominously at me. I picked it up, not with a sense of compassion, but with a sense of horror and dread. Due to its resin coating, it was impossible to burn, so I wrapped it up in a white satin cloth, placed it in a container and covered it with salt. I carried out a little ritual to rid myself of whatever curse this object possessed. Then I

---

*An extrusive igneous rock. It is occurring as a natural glass formed by the rapid cooling of viscous lava from volcanoes. (https://geologyscience.com/minerals/obsidian)

used sage incense over it and dug a hole. I placed it in the ground next to where I had buried one of my beloved cats. For a few days things seemed normal; until more other-worldly experiences started.

Cheri and I began to smell tobacco, as if someone had recently smoked a cigarette; it was increasing in its frequency and intensity. There was also a strange roar – like that of a dragon – that seemed to be flying over the house and, to top it off, I was awoken one evening by a strange sound coming from the kitchen. My heart was beating at a thousand paces as I crept down the hallway. My little dog was snoring blissfully, totally unaware of what I heard. Shaking, I continued to hear the sound as I crept ever closer to the source. I could detect its presence on the kitchen bench as its shrill tone continued. As I reached the corner – in direct line of where it came from – it ceased abruptly. I froze. I thought I was about to be attacked. I fumbled for something to shield myself with and scrabbled for the kitchen light switch. The light dazzled me. There was absolutely nothing there.

How bizarre! I thought as I stumbled back to bed. I looked at the clock – 3.11am. That number 11 again, I noted as I tried to rationalise what I was experiencing. Since 2011, I had not been able to sleep through the night. I woke every couple of hours – usually between the hours of 2.00 am and 4.00 am. When I would check the time, there was usually the number 11 in the sequence, or the numbers added up to 11. As I had previously researched the number and its meaning, I wondered what the Universe was trying to show me.

The next morning as I cleaned the kitchen benches, I noticed a pile of something sitting near where the eerie noise had emanated. What I initially interpreted as kitchen debris soon presented as having a finer dust – akin to moon dust. The particles were like tiny pieces of fine ash; they risked being blown away and they had a decidedly earthy smell. Whatever or whomever had made their presence known last night appeared to want me to acknowledge their existence and to confirm that I did not dream what I had heard. My rational mind, however, continued to override the possibility of 'something unknown'. I grabbed the dustpan and brush and sent the stardust packing out into the front yard where its weightlessness caused it to vanish.

The other-worldly interruptions continued with strange humming noises and ghostly encounters. These occurrences were often at night when I was asleep. I had often felt I was being touched on the head and, in meditation, those soft feather-like touches caressed my face as if to reassure me.

A young girl would often appear in my bedroom at night. I thought it was Cheri and I had called out to her. I studied her features and long hair and, convinced it was her, would stagger out of bed to find no-one there. Had she been sleepwalking and gone back to bed? In the morning Cheri had no recollection of such events. What also puzzled me, was that Cheri was no longer a little girl but was now a young adult; that did not fit the appearance of the presence I had seen.

Cheri and I had always been energetically connected. I once remember meditating and being given a series of numbers in a download. As I came out of my trance state to write them down, an excited Cheri came out of her room to inform me of a series of numbers she had just envisioned.

"Quickly," I said, "write them down."

To my amazement it was the same sequence of numbers I had just transposed! I kept them for a long time pondering what they could mean, even using them for Gold Lotto a few times. Cheri was also highly gifted psychically and could pick a number out of a series of three cards in a deck with 100 per cent accuracy.

As a young child, Cheri would often experience déjà vu – the feeling of having experienced something previously that you have never done before – or be somewhere for the first time and feeling an uncanny sense of familiarity. Often, we would be travelling when she would insist she had been there before and would point out various landmarks. At other times she would be playing and, as if transported to another reality, would declare she had a feeling of experiencing the scenario many times before. Often, she would be ecstatic, living the most wondrous experience of the most divine sweet smell which could only be described as coming from heaven.

"The angels are with you!" I would reply. "This is their calling card – so whenever you feel sad remember they are never far from your side."

Cheri was an exceptional, positive and optimistic child until puberty arrived and this, along with a diagnosis of autism, changed her perception of the world into one of negativity. She found she was unable to mix socially with her schoolmates and she found the education system stifling. She became depressed.

It was then I realised the more negative Cheri became, the more the unusual activity in the house escalated. Was something feeding off her low energy? More and more portals opened up in the house and began to spread down the hallway and into all the rooms. Cheri was a huge fan of *Game of Thrones* and this became her release from the world and society. When she was not working, she would spend hours watching the series. She also purchased all types of memorabilia, including the three sigils related to the kingdoms: The lion, wolf and dragon.

It was not long before another shape began to appear, but this time in Cheri's room. A white apparition developed beneath the *Game of Thrones* dragon sigil, and it had morphed into – you guessed it – the shape of a dragon.

Clearly visible were the backbone, ribcage and pelvis in this reptilian entity. However, its head was more like that of a human, with a large elongated skull. I stood mesmerised as I studied it. It maintained an upright position and, although lizard-like, seemed eerily human. Strangely, my family could also clearly see it; every detail of the vertebral column could be seen. Was it trying to provide a clue to something that was difficult to fathom in a rational way?

As if that was not enough, the same being showed up on the window, only this time the image was more of the thoracic spine and ribcage. Every vertebra could be seen quite clearly, together with the ribcage. *What is the meaning behind accentuating this anatomy?* I wondered as I studied its fine detail. *What is the message behind all of this? Could the clues lead me to the answer?* As I gazed at this image of a thorax, I noticed there were twelve vertebrae and, although it was difficult to count the ribs, I was beginning to think that perhaps this was a humanoid image rather than that of a lizard.

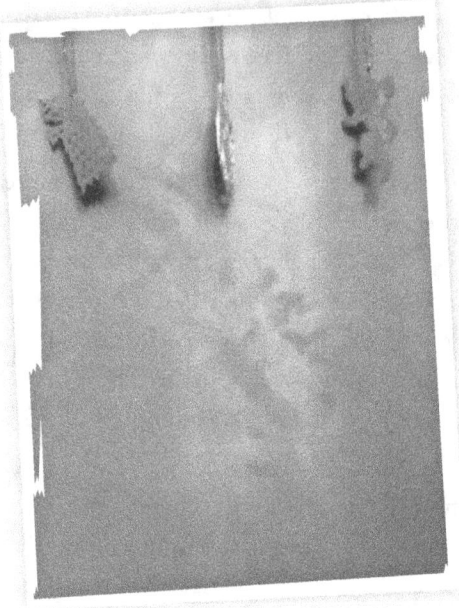

Apparition on wall near Game of Thrones dragon sigel

My love of crystals became a passion at that time, as I began to study their properties. It was not long before a piece of rhodolite attracted my attention whilst shopping. With its delicious rosy appearance, I asked to hold it in my hand and, instantly, it began to resonate with my energetic field.

"I will take this one," I said, as I placed it in my handbag. I did not know – yet again – an inanimate object would result in communication to the most amazing beings; and the introduction to one in particular, who would become my guardian in other worlds.

As I settled down to meditate with my beautiful new rhodolite crystal, I felt my hand pulsing and synchronising with the rock as if it was trying to communicate with me. I opened my eyes and, in a state of trance, stared at the lounge room window. The window appeared to take on a life of its own. In the glass appeared a man of Indigenous appearance; his eyes seemed to pierce straight through me. He looked like a medicine man/shaman and appeared stern and steadfast, as if deep in thought and contemplation. Every time our eyes met, the rock would pulse rhythmically in my hand, almost as if sending a Morse code message.

I rubbed my eyes thinking they were playing tricks on me. The image then morphed into the most magnificent regal lion. Its eyes glowed majestically, its fabulous royal mane and prestigious presence evident. Again, as our eyes locked, the rock would pulse with some form of hidden message. Frustratingly, I could not understand it.

Every day after this amazing experience the lion/man would appear on one of the windows or glass doors as if sending a greeting. Sometimes I wiped the image away as my rational mind decided that my brain had been affected by a virus and it must be an optical illusion. Every time I wiped it away, within 24 hours it would return; it did not want to be erased from my memory. I decided to see if I could draw the representation before me, as no-one else could see anything on the window remotely like a lion/man, or any other shape. They quickly came to the conclusion that it was migraine-related and dismissed my impassioned descriptions of it.

I am no artist, but something – divine intervention? – took hold and I sketched the most magnificent lion/man. With a prominent nose and leonine appearance, he wore a bejewelled turban suggestive of his regal presence. In my mind the name Bashar seemed fitting. In Hebrew and Arabic this name means 'Bringer of Glad Tidings'. I had never felt a kinship like this – with my imaginary friend – and felt sure he was a messenger of some kind. I hoped all of the strange activity in the house were meant to reveal good intentions.

It was not long before other shapes began to appear on the windows, as if I had given permission for others to make their presence known. Next was Nimrod: Avian, with beady eyes and feathers. He had crazy bushy eyebrows, like a human with a small mouth and prominent chin, but instead of a beak he had a small pert nose. He had a magnificent comb on his head – like that of a rooster – but his sparkled like gold.

Next came Suzz who reminded me of a cross between a cat and the sloth in *The Lion King*. He had gangly limbs, a prominent nose, an elegant long neck and the slanty eyes of a cat. The two tufts of short fur on his head resembled a pair of ears.

Last but not least was Sam. Like a genie from *Aladdin's Cave*, he was menacing with a mesmerising stare and a round chubby face, a black beard and a turban. He looked as if he could disappear in a puff of smoke. Every time I glanced at the window, he seemed to read every move. I started to feel decidedly uncomfortable with this motley mix of creatures, and with a swift wipe of the window, banished them to history. Only Bashar remained a constant who continued to materialise regularly.

Am I going mad? I asked as I pondered my sketches of these other-worldly beings. My family thought I had just made them up, but I know they had been in my reality at that moment of space and time.

Sketch of Bashar – my lion/shaman

I adjusted to living with each strange event even though it was all becoming rather surreal. Although the large male hand had stopped appearing on the mirror, sometimes a more feminine one, with soft delicate features, would replace the masculine one. Still an ill fit for either Cheri's or my hand, it obviously had its own statement to make.

As Cheri slept soundly, a female voice abruptly ended her slumber. Shaken, disorientated and unable to interpret what the voice was communicating, Cheri brushed it off as part of a dream. When she described this to me, I felt a sense of unease, given the emergence of a large skeletal hand the night prior to Cheri's car accident. Could this be another warning of trouble ahead? It was not long before a message behind the visitation was revealed.

Late in the evening, Cheri began to feel decidedly unwell. Complaining of a headache and pain in her back, she ran a high fever. Home remedy endeavours to relieve the pain proved futile and her condition deteriorated before me. She had severe chest pain and a forbidding purple rash began to creep over parts of her body. **Warning, warning!** my brain screamed. I immediately realised what this meant. Her blood was being poisoned and her internal organs were shutting down. She was being invaded by some insidious bacteria.

Shaking uncontrollably and on the verge of unconsciousness, Cheri was rushed to hospital. It was found she had an untreated urinary tract infection resulting in septicaemia. Intravenous antibiotics and a couple of days in hospital meant she was on the road to recovery. Thank goodness we sought medical treatment quickly. I could not help thinking how easily she could have died, and whether the ominous voice in the dark of the night was a foreboding.

It seems – since I spoke to the old man under the bed – that 'talking to the dead' is one of my innate gifts. My deceased brother came to me in a visitation – one of my lucid dreams. He was driving a car and I was the passenger. We were on a winding country road with beautiful glowing scenery. We talked for some time on subjects I have no recollection of, but towards the end of the dream, he stopped the car and turned to me –

his eyes were black as the strange gift of obsidian. There was no colour or joy in his eyes; they were ill-matched to the brilliance of the landscape we had experienced. I was horrified and abruptly ended the dream.

My interpretation of this was – since he had passed away in a traumatic and unexpected manner – my brother was lost in the astral plane and could not understand how to progress. I must have helped him move on, as a few weeks later he reappeared in my dreams and his sparkling bright blue eyes had returned. Although no telepathic exchange occurred this time, I felt reassured that he had gone into the higher planes of existence as pure love.

It was not long after this that one of my dear friends lost her husband to brain cancer. I had not been shocked by his illness as, some months prior to his diagnosis, he came in one of my lucid dreams in the form of Santa Claus. With his big round face and chubby red cheeks – and what looked like a red beanie – I thought it hilarious and told his wife. However, what appeared to be an innocent dream turned out to be an ominous prediction. The cherubic features were the result of chemotherapy and steroids causing his face to swell disproportionately to the rest of his body, and the red beanie was not a Santa hat: He wore it because of hair loss.

If only I could interpret the meaning behind the dreams before the event occurs. I have come to realise that I am tapping into the universal consciousness in such a way that I become entangled in the collective energies of others. This is not to change destinies, but to show that we are all part of the one big quantum soup known as the Universe.

I was expecting a visitation following his journey to the other side, and was amazed at how quickly I received a sign. Whilst at the funeral I decided not to go to the graveside, so wandered around trying in vain to find the wake venue. I went to leave. The car would not start. I managed to get it going after some coaxing and, as I drove out of the funeral home's driveway the car spluttered again. Must be some bad fuel in the line. Then the dashboard went crazy! Dials went up and down and a strange vibration sounded. Was it trying to get my attention?

It stopped as soon as it had started, and I continued my journey. It happened again, halfway down the road. I pulled into the local mechanic who, after close inspection, could not find anything wrong. The next day the car was purring along as if nothing had ever happened. However, I know in my heart that it was my friend's husband letting me know that he was OK. He loved all things mechanical, and it made me smile to know this was his cheeky response to my leaving the funeral service early. Even the deceased have a sense of humour!

CHAPTER FIVE

The Shamanic Way

The weirdness continued. 'Things that go bump in the night' became a regular occurrence. Most nights I would wake between 1.00 am and 3.00 am, usually to the sound of footsteps on the roof. *The possums must have heavy boots on*, I thought, and dismissed this disruption to my sleep. However, as the weeks passed, I noticed something strange. The disturbance would occur at relatively the same time every night; the footsteps a consistent rhythm only carried out on a certain section of the roof.

It became like clockwork, as if there was indeed some entity that came alive and, as if powered by some unseen force, could only walk in one direction. It always came from above my bedroom ceiling and never went anywhere near the other side of the house where Cheri was sleeping. It seemed as if it walked in a grid, sometimes completing the task just once, but often two or three times.

It was not long before the night-time roof dance began to ramp up. It consistently woke me on the hour every hour and, when I looked at the time, the number would always appear with either 11 or would add up to 11. Bashar, my shaman, continued to make his presence known on the mirror. As I sat up in bed to ponder this, I concluded there must be a connection between the two.

I thought: *Is the entity on the roof the shaman I see in my mind's eye in the mirror, and if so, what is the urgent message he is trying to invoke?* Intuitively I felt that whatever being this represented, they were performing a type of ritual to protect me in some way – perhaps from negative entities I also felt were present in the house.

I decided to follow a shamanic ritual in my daily meditation and asked the shaman for help so I could obtain a greater understanding of this strange presence. One night, in my lucid state, I became aware of a series of golden glyphs falling from the sky into my mind's eye. Sparkling in their honey-colour, they danced in harmonious procession and expressed themselves in a language of light.

Buoyed on by the messages both while asleep and awake I felt in my heart that I did indeed communicate with my shaman, Bashar. I decided to ask the pendulum the question of my higher consciousness – *Is this what I know to be true?* I received a resounding 'Yes'. My rational mind, however, still continued its intrusive thoughts of *You are deluding yourself if you think you are connecting with someone* and *A pendulum is never 100 per cent accurate.*

I decided to see if I could also get a sign through my meditations. After carrying out a shamanic ritual and holding my favourite rhodolite crystal, the apparition once again appeared on the window. This time I tried to channel an answer and I got a most unexpected response. As I entered deeper into the meditation, I cleared my third eye and asked the question: *Are you the shaman that walks on the roof?* No response. But after a few minutes, unconsciously my head began to move in an up and down motion resembling the pendulum giving a "Yes".

Do you mean me any harm? I asked. After a few minutes the response was a sideways turning of the head, the pendulum's "No".

Are you my protector?

"Yes", was the quick response.

I cannot explain why my head decided to turn in those directions when I posed the questions; I only knew that it was out of my conscious control and I was not intentionally making the movements. I decided to experiment by asking other questions of the pendulum – and then in deep meditation – to see if the answers to the question were the same. I always got a similar response. I decided it was just part of my freakish self and added it to the list of other weird happenings such as the water and electricity phenomena.

My enquiring mind, however, still wanted answers so I decided I had to ask Bashar if he could communicate with me again in my dream state. It was not long before I was receiving not only Egyptian glyphs, but also what I could only describe as grid patterns with a decidedly Indigenous look. There would be feathers and earthy stones arranged in such a way as if to transmit knowledge. They would appear fleetingly in my third eye, and then disappear. The stones and other objects seemed very old and what I was visioning felt so real – as if I was somewhere in another time and space, performing some type of ritual.

As the grid pattern began to appear regularly, my intuition was drawn yet again to the little duck I had buried in the backyard. *What could the significance of that duck be?* Ever inquisitive, I searched the meaning of ducks from a spiritual perspective.

Like other birds, ducks fly in the sky and swoop down onto the earth and onto water. This indicated that they are happy in two worlds. Spiritually, water relates to emotions, so maybe I needed to examine my emotions more deeply. Ducks are also happy to ground themselves, whereas I have difficulty with the harsh earth environment.

OK, I thought. *What am I avoiding, and is this resistance preventing me from moving on in life? Is the shaman trying to convey a message via this craggy old duck?*

I began to consider that the shaman was acting as a bridge between the upper and lower worlds. My protector and guide, the duck totem, was sent to wake me up to something that, up until now, I had not been aware of. *Did the shaman utilise an animate object to open up my consciousness* to something other than this material 3D existence? And if so, why had I been chosen?

What about the symbols on the ceiling? What message were they trying to convey? They were obviously a language of sorts and, as I gazed intently, the long flute-like lines reminded me of water and the fluidity of life. Suddenly 'go with the flow' and the words 'yin and yang' sprang to mind. Was the universal message here about the masculine and feminine aspects of energy and the ability to embrace the duality of both? So many questions and yet I still did not have the answers.

It had been some months now since I found the little duck on the driveway. All these bizarre incidents had occurred since its discovery. I had gotten used to the creepy hand marks and other signs on the windows and ceilings, but what was to come played havoc with my sanity.

For two or three nights in succession, I was wakened by the shrill sound of the smoke alarm. I checked that nothing was alight in the house; all was well. Every hour on the hour the incessant beeping would start, and I would again check the house to find – nothing. I determined the battery must be failing and thought nothing more of it. The next day I changed the battery and replaced the alarm only to be woken again to beeping which still occurred every hour, like clockwork.

After three nights of sleep deprivation, I was desperate and decided to have the smoke alarm checked. No issues and the battery fully charged. *Just like Morse code, what was the message behind the beeping?* I thought, as I struggled to make sense of it. I asked the shaman for some clarity. His roof-walk began not only to occur once in the night but as if he was on patrol 24/7. Sleep time was ever more eventful. After a couple of nights of the continuous robotic dance on the roof, the beeping stopped and all was well.

Is Bashar protecting me from another unseen force? I often felt there was more than one entity in the house. I would look up to see a puff of black smoke appear in the air, only to disappear immediately. I had recorded some course notes from some lectures I had been listening to, only to find when I replayed them, they had been wiped and a strange guttural noise could be heard, as if someone was clearing their throat.

I also noticed that the hand marks were spreading throughout the whole house and also onto my car. When I wiped the marks off the car that familiar pungent earthy smell would return, as if protesting my interference. I wondered if Bashar had arranged to place the obsidian under Cheri's car that day in order to protect her from some dark force. Why, oh why, did I not keep the stones? They were obviously meant as some sort of protection. Obsidian is a grounding stone, so perhaps it was also a message to me to ground myself to the earth for greater protection.

So began a series of aura cleanses, and I placed my bare feet into the earth each day. I loved the feel of the warm earth and imagined I was growing roots from my feet to help anchor and support me. I noticed it helped with the constant disequilibrium and wondered if some of my vestibular symptoms were of a spiritual origin.

One day, as I lay down on the bed, I looked up at the ceiling to find a grid symbol – a crosshatch – directly above my head. It seemed my bedroom was the next target for these curious symbols. Whilst shopping one day in a bookstore, I browsed the New Age section and a book on numerology took my interest. As I flipped through the pages, I came across the same crosshatch grid that appeared above my head on the bedroom ceiling. With my fascination for numbers, particularly the number 11, I purchased the numerology book and began to teach myself how to chart an individual's unique numerology profile based on their name and birth details.

I put together charts for a few friends who found the results to be true. When completing my own, I was enlightened to find – based on the same symbolic grid on the ceiling – I was spiritually top-heavy; I lacked emphasis on the material earthly aspects of life. My lesson in this life, therefore, was to find a balance between embracing the spiritual aspects without negating the material world with all of its blessings and sufferings.

As I pondered my emotional state, I began to consider how introverted I had become; years of bullying and oppression had worn me down. I no longer socialised frequently and had a small group of friends. The episodes of vertigo and other ascension symptoms had taken their toll on my self-esteem. I had been left with a rigid and less spontaneous approach to life. I had to agree: I was stuck in a quagmire of negativity and material pursuits now brought little joy or comfort. I had removed myself from the enjoyment of beautiful things, preferring to concentrate on spiritual advancement. I had not bought myself any interesting new clothes in years, and I had forgotten the inner child who loved to play dress-ups and wear beautiful jewellery. I looked in the mirror and could barely recognise myself following the bizarre awakening that began in 2011. It was as if my previous soul had left my body and something else had taken over; in spiritual terms this is called a 'walk-in'.

My meditation friend told me that, when a soul goes through constant abuse and trauma and can no longer tolerate its current situation, arrangements are made with the higher conscious for another soul to take its place. Years of ill health, bullying, financial stress and relationship struggles had taken their toll and I no longer viewed the world as a beautiful place. I sometimes felt desperate to leave this body and struggled to experience joy and happiness. During this awakening process I had aged dramatically. My soulless self had lost its sense of purpose.

But how to get me back? I wondered. *How to live on this earthly plane when life can be such a struggle?*

"See beyond the suffering and recognise your own power," said my meditation friend.

OK. I decided to splash out on an updated wardrobe and hairstyle, and caught up with friends for coffee. Although it was a major boost to my self-esteem, I still could not erase that feeling – which had haunted me since birth – of not belonging.

I began to feel a sense of unease, particularly when alone in the house. As I only worked part-time I was often at home by myself. On one particular day I was in the laundry sorting the clothes when I heard a tremendous roaring noise. *Where on earth is that coming from?* I left the laundry to investigate. I reached the entrance to the toilet and my eyes widened in astonishment.

"Oh, my lord!" I cried in panic. I could not believe what I was witnessing. The toilet was making strange gurgling noises – as if it had just swallowed a giant beast. As I adjusted to this aberration, the toilet seat began to judder and the gurgling noises intensified. What monster could make that guttural sound?

What happened next was beyond anything I had ever experienced. The toilet seat, which had been vibrating incessantly, now began to thrash up and down. If that was not enough, the toilet's walls began to have contractions – violent waves – as if giving birth to something from another dimension.

My eyes were as big as saucers, while my mind tried to grasp what I witnessed. My heart pounded as my flight or fight response kicked in. I had no choice but to flee. I grabbed my phone and bolted outside with the thought the house might implode at any moment. As I cowered at the front of the house, my rational mind took charge and I wondered if, perhaps, a burst pipe was the culprit and that water would eventually flood the house. Should I ring the local council? My hands shook as I tried to dial the number – but I could not get a connection.

I decided to investigate to see if any water was escaping into the house. Trembling, I crept through to the kitchen. The roaring was still audible but there was no evidence of water. I sat down and rang my husband. Still shaking, I was relieved when he answered.

"What's up?" he asked.

"Get a load of this," I replied in a shrill voice, as I walked down the hallway to the toilet where the roaring and gurgling was as loud as ever. "Can you hear it? Can you hear it?" I screeched "What the hell do you think this is?" I put the phone on speaker. As I held the phone closer to the source, the noise abruptly stopped.

I could not believe it. The tsunami-like movements of the walls ceased and the crazy toilet seat antics fell silent.

"What am I supposed to be listening to?" he asked matter-of-factly.

I needed reassurance and tried to explain what had occurred. Could it have been a gas or water leak?

He was non-committal about my story as he had seen plenty of proof that something strange was happening in the house. He tried to reassure me as best he could. "Maybe something got stuck in the sewer line," he proposed. But this did not account for the inexplicable wall contortions, let alone the dancing toilet seat!

I felt like *Alice in Wonderland*. Had I gone down the rabbit hole? I began to question my sanity.

"Before you go – could you please hang on whilst I try flushing the toilet just in case it happens again?" I asked reluctantly. I needed to pee, so I mustered up enough courage to place my bootie on the seat. Would it turn into a crazy mad hatter dance? Nothing out of the ordinary happened. I envisaged some fiend coming up from the bowels of the sewer to engulf me and suck me down the gurgler... Like when I was a child and sat on the thunderbox waiting for the bogie man to get me.

Nothing happened. As I relaxed and released my bladder, I noticed a strange black mark that looked like soot on the wall in front of me. OK, let's see what happens when I flush the toilet. As I pressed the button, I wondered if the walls would open up and I would be engulfed in a sea of water – but again, nothing happened.

I examined the strange black mark closely. It looked like a symbol and was definitely not there before the incident. It looked as if the energy, or force that was attempting to come through the walls and toilet, had succeeded and had left its energy-imprint as a sign.

I was frightened of being alone in the house and I hesitantly told the story of my extraordinary encounter to my work colleagues. I was expecting a casual reaction, but was surprised when one of the female medical staff reached out in concern for my welfare. The woman knew someone who could perform a house-cleansing ritual and suggested I make contact.

'Fred' I had been told, could perform a ritual to remove the entity from the house and, when I asked if he could make a home visit, I was surprised to find that this would not be necessary.

"I remote-view, so I do not have to be there in person," he replied straightforwardly. "Just give me the exact address of your establishment and I will enter your premises."

How fascinating, I thought. How could someone so far away know what was going on in my house? Feeling a little awkward, and somewhat sceptical of this endeavour, I was given a prayer to recite to receive protection from Archangel Michael. I was told to repeat the prayer three times at exactly 8.00 pm and then to go to sleep for the rest of the evening. On waking the following day, I was instructed to ring back at 3.00 pm to report.

Sheepishly, I walked around the rooms to see if there was any evidence of disturbance. All seemed in place and for the first time in weeks the dreaded smoke alarm had not intruded into my sleep. I rang 'Fred' at 3.00 pm and told him the smoke detector had remained silent but that I could not detect if anything else had changed. "That is OK," he replied, "I am fairly sure that you will have no further issues."

I was curious about the mischievous offender and asked 'who' or 'what' had been residing in the house. I was not expecting such a terse reply. 'Fred' informed me that it was not in my best interests to know. I pushed further and was told that there was a battle of the dark and the light. I still did not understand. He said I must protect my purity at all costs. Without revealing what he knew, he told me I needed to keep the good ones in the house and the bad ones outside.

"They have been having a party at your expense and I have removed the freeloaders. Do not sage inside the house as you want to encourage 'the protectors' to stay."

'Fred' promptly ended the conversation by saying, "If you have any further issues, just let me know and I will toss them out again." He hung up abruptly.

Wow! What a revelation this had been. However, I could not help wonder why he would not tell me the truth of the origins of the mysterious entities. It made sense that there were both dark and light forces at work, but I was still not convinced that the so-called malevolent ones were indeed bad. That night, Cheri was woken by a loud mournful sound – as if someone was in pain. Half asleep and straining to hear where the noise was coming from, she looked outside her bedroom window. The mournful cries continued and then she gasped: there was a sound of someone violently whacking my car with a hard object.

Cheri froze, and prayed that 'whatever was out there' would not smash her bedroom window. Finally, there was silence and she slipped back to sleep. The next morning, Cheri hurried to the window to look outside.

"What?"

She raced outside to have a good look and was surprised to find no damage to my beloved car. Cheri woke me to tell the tale and, as we both examined the car for evidence, I noticed a pattern of 'creepy hands' in a trail on the bonnet.

It seems my reptilian friends had been booted out of the house so I asked myself the following questions:

★ *Why were they so bad that 'Fred' had them removed?*

★ *Why would they let out such mournful emotional cries, as if grieving the loss of their newfound abode and from our energy?*

Despite the frightening toilet incident, I had a strange familiarity with their presence – as if we were somehow connected to each other.

My thoughts returned to the unaffected car; Cheri continued to insist it had been deliberately smashed. I remembered the time when I was involved in the ute incident, where I switched realities and my car was saved. Could it be that she had switched timelines so my car would be saved, yet again, from a similar fate? So many questions. Maybe Cheri was dreaming at the time and thought she heard something – yet the handprints stared back at me from the paintwork reminding me that unseen presences were still at work.

All became quiet in the house for the first time in ages. It seemed 'Fred' really had managed to remove whatever had taken up residence in the household. No more creepy hands and 'things that go bump in the night', but Bashar remained a constant in my life. He continued to appear on the mirror and provide his usual moves on the rooftop. We decided not to paint over the unusual markings, and left them there as a reminder of the world unseen. Besides, one did not want to disturb the energy that might permit a portal into the house.

I had always wondered if there was a series of energy grids or ley lines underneath the house that had attracted these forces. I also considered one of the psychic's responses to my situation: She felt my house sat on top of an important Indigenous site, and that my shaman was a traditional elder who roamed this area hundreds of years ago. She had also spoken of cat spirits trying to get my attention by knocking things over.

I had owned two beautiful chinchilla Persian cats for many years. When our dog, Englebert, died, Booz, the male cat, gave me warning of his own forthcoming departure, and also a sign he was now in the afterlife. Booz had been sick for quite a while and, when we obtained our new puppy to replace Englebert, he became more dismayed and decided it was time to leave. On the morning of his demise, he ate very little and attracted my attention by talking incessantly in his adorable cat language. As he stared intently into my eyes, I felt a sense of urgency in his vocalisations and, just like when I knew my own mamma was ill, I realised he was saying goodbye. I gently caressed and hugged my beloved mate and silently told him it was OK for him to go.

Late that evening he had not come in for dinner and, despite calling and searching, Booz could not be found. We held out hope for a few days, but it was clear he had left home to die elsewhere, as cats often do. About a week later we all heard his distinctive meow coming from outside. Was he trapped somewhere? Stuck in a drain perhaps? But despite our efforts we could not find him. A few days later all communication ceased. I had looked after my beloved Booz for almost twelve years and had an intimate understanding of his cat language. I believe the vocals we heard were not a cry of distress but a sign that all was OK as he entered the spirit world.

My other Persian cat, Priscilla, did not have it so easy when she departed the earthly plane. Demented, blind and struggling to eat and walk, she curled up in a ball waiting to die. She was in and out of consciousness for a few days as we tried to ease her distress as much as possible until she eventually passed. All of our pets had transitioned via a natural death; my emotions were heavy as I wondered if we should have had her put down. I reminded myself that she had a good life, and had lived to sixteen years of age. I hoped I would get a sign from her soon that she was now OK and living her best cat life elsewhere.

Unlike Englebert and Booz before her, the weeks passed with still no sign from Priscilla. Of all of our pets she had been my favourite fur baby. Weeks and months passed, and I wondered why she had not left a sign of her passing as the other pets had. It would take nine years to hear from her again.

The plumbing in our older house had been inefficient for some time and the pipe from the sink kept blocking up. Eventually we called in a plumber. After an inspection the diagnosis was that we needed extra plumbing and a drainage trap. The line would run from the kitchen, out the back of the house precisely where Priscilla had been laid to rest – coincidentally, next to the beady-eyed duck.

I thought no more of the synchronicity and, as I washed up one evening, I distinctly heard rather urgent cat cries coming from the direction of the front door. I chose to ignore the situation thinking it was a feral cat having an altercation with another stray. However, the cry was so distinctive and I realised that this was not just any cry, but that of my beloved Priscilla! I raced to the front door, opened it, and there in the distance stood a ghostly apparition: A beautiful long-haired white cat. The crying immediately stopped as I recognised my adored animal. She looked happy and, most importantly, healthy, as telepathically I was told that she was now free to enter the spirit world having been trapped for so long. She then vanished, never to appear again.

It seems that, due to her traumatic death, she was stuck between worlds, becoming trapped in the earthly plane. I wondered if somehow the plumber had sufficiently disturbed the energy grids underneath the house to open up a portal for her to escape to other realms. Did she obtain assistance from the little duck, or are there other entities living underground that aided her escape? Was the psychic correct in suggesting the knocking over of ornaments was deceased cat spirits? Perhaps it was

Booz attempting to get my attention that all was not well with Priscilla. Whatever the reason I was so grateful I got to see her one last time, and that I can now rest easy that she is once more with Booz and Englebert.

Have you ever been visited by beloved animals after they passed from this life? Write your experiences here.

CHAPTER SIX

Interdimensional Travels and the Jean Effect

Despite the house returning to some sort of normality, I could not stop reflecting on the past twelve months. Although I was grateful to 'Fred' for intervening and helping me cope, I still yearned to know why this had happened to me. I felt a sense of aloneness as there really was no-one I knew who had experienced similar events. It also did not help that 'Fred' refused to divulge critical information that might have helped me come to terms with the still hidden and unknown. Strangely, I could not erase the feeling of loss. It was as if banishing the unearthly entities was in effect banishing myself from a truth that needed to be told.

I decided to begin my own research into interstellar beings and was surprised to find much hidden knowledge that has been kept from the general public. I learned about the alien races that have visited this planet for thousands of years and their connections to historic places such as the pyramids in Egypt and Stonehenge in England. I read about spaceships, and portals to the stars, and the hybridisation of humans with extraterrestrial beings. I was particularly fascinated by the literature saying those who possess the RH factor may be seeded from an unknown source.

My daughter and I have RH negative blood and I was excited to find that this blood type also has similar physical characteristics: a reddish tinge to the hair, pale skin and eyes, low body temperature, sensitivity to light and sound. And, most surprising, an extra appendage such as a rib or tailbone. I had all of these, including a spare rib. My reading revealed that it is also known as alien blood as it was thought that it was 'the blood of the gods' – the Anunnaki – who visited Earth from the sky and were seen as royalty.

Cheri's father has RH positive blood, so there was concern she may have been born with her father's blood system. This would have required a blood transfusion to counteract the effects of the two bloods mixing. Luckily, she was born RH negative and has some of the traits of this blood system. When she was a baby, her little body would be so cold that her lips would turn blue. Her temperature would fall to 34° Celsius, despite keeping her body warm and snug. One particularly cold night I was concerned enough to ring the hospital outpatients, only to be told that she could not possibly have a temperature that low and it was time I purchased a new thermometer! The childcare centre would often comment how low her temperature was, but a thorough investigation by the medical fraternity ruled out any hidden diseases.

As I delved further, I read about alien beings from other star systems and constellations. There were the Lyrans with cat-like features, the Arcturans with their slender blue bodies, and the Pleiadeans with their beautiful Scandinavian humanoid features, amongst many. The aliens, however, that made my eyes turn into flying saucers – excuse the pun – were the reptilians from the Draco constellation. As I stared at their features, I realised they had some similar markings to the ones found on the walls and windows. Could it be that there was an other-worldly connection to these creatures and that was why I felt a sense of sadness at their departure?

But wait!

Continuing my research, I found these particular aliens had not been very friendly to others in the galaxy, and they had initiated many planetary wars. As a peace-loving individual, I found it hard to conceive I could possibly have been seeded from such an aggressive species. My monkey mind was immediately shut down by my rational mind. It determined this was just a deluded fantasy and, to put it bluntly, **a whole load of hogwash!**

I decided to unplug myself from *Close Encounters of the Third Kind* and look for courses that would continue to enhance my journey through the ascension process. Despite everything, my disequilibrium persisted, although some other symptoms had finally dissipated. I was particularly interested in ways of managing the emotional and physical aspects of this awakening process and, as I utilised the internet, I was guided to a fascinating site on medical intuition.

Medical Intuition – this looks noteworthy, I thought, as I read about the self and how our emotions can affect various body parts. I read all about chakras, ancestral patterning, DNA recoding, quantum energy and the merkaba* and was blown away. I had been on the spiritual path for quite some time, but this information brought it to a whole new level. I was particularly drawn to the owner and teacher of this curriculum – Jean – whose dark brown eyes held a glint of things to come.

I decided to call Jean to discuss a booking. I spoke to her, and felt immediate rapport, but was still uncertain whether this was the right decision. Jean suggested I read her autobiography and offered to post a complimentary copy. What a revelation! When it arrived, I had finished it within the day. I knew I had found a kindred spirit. Jean had experienced the awakening process, and confirmed she had experienced – and witnessed – what she lovingly called 'the dudes'. It was not long before I was back on the phone to her, excitedly blurting out my experiences with 'the dudes' and being eternally grateful for somebody who got it.

I booked in for a weekend course. It was wonderful to learn about the chakras and how they affect our bodily organs, and also how the seasons affect us. The five elements: Fire, earth, metal, water and wood also play a huge role. Of more importance were the concepts around gratitude, abundance and self-love. In order to remove emotional blocks and negative self-talk it was necessary to remove old thought patterns and connect more fully with our higher self. Through medical intuitive

*Merkaba: Spiritual ascension techniques.

techniques, meditation, breath and movement, by the end of the weekend I was even more motivated to take the next course.

The next course arrived and we talked about the ascension process and the awakening to higher consciousness through the experience of kundalini. We learnt about crystal gridding techniques, and now it was time to work on each other in pairs. It was decided that I would be the recipient of an energetic exchange through my lovely nominated partner, with whom I felt an instant connection. As she placed the gorgeous lemurian crystals on my belly, I was asked to take a deep breath. As her hand hovered above my solar plexus, immediately my body began to gyrate and contort as if I was trying to stop something from happening.

What the hell!

The next thing I knew, I was wailing uncontrollably like a wounded animal. Part of me was aware of my surroundings, but another part was somewhere else, recalling an obviously painful situation. Several attempts to help me breathe through the experience proved unsuccessful until eventually, as the wailing became more intense, I was forced to abandon the session.

After a short time recovering, I pondered the experience with the rest of the class. My thoughts led me to suggest that I was remembering a birth process and, for whatever reason, I did not wish to be born. *Would this explain the wild muscle contorting, was it my resistance to travel down the birth canal? Why did I not want to be born? I thought about it for days*; and then my heart directed me to the answer. Straight away, I spoke out loud, "Because I did not want to leave my twin."

Oh my God! The twin flame connection? What is that?

I discovered twin flames share deep and powerful spiritual connections and they share the same soul consciousness. They choose to separate and reincarnate many times on the earthly plane in order to learn the ultimate lesson of self-love. They also need to experience the illusion of separation so they can finally end their karmic patterns and reunite as one. This is not about yearning for romantic love, but more about finding the divine love within themselves.

It is rare that twin flames reunite on the earthly plane, but with the new awakening and dawning of the Age of Aquarius many couples have worked through all of their energetic blockages. They have raised their vibrations sufficiently to recognise and appreciate all aspects of each other – individually and collectively – and have now come to act as a mirror for others in order that they, too, become part of the new human consciousness.

There are those, however, who will continue to lead separate lives, even though they may have reincarnated at the same time, and even at the same location. One may feel an instant attraction to their beloved – as if they have come home – but the other is totally unaware of their true connection. Therefore, one becomes the chaser and the other the runner, with the conscious party constantly feeling the loss of the other. Incidentally, the 11:11 numbering is not only part of the ascension awakening, but also symbolises the twin flame connection: The embodiment of the feminine and masculine as one. *Could the mournful wailing have been the sense of desolation and isolation of being parted from a twin flame? One who exists somewhere in a different reality and that, once again, without whom I was forced to continue another lifetime?*

But could there be more to the story of my traumatic experience?

I stumbled across Delores Cannon's convoluted universe books and realised through her revelations with hypnosis and other rebirthing techniques that, not only have we lived many lives on this earthly plane, but we have also existed in other dimensions and galaxies. I was fascinated to learn that there are multiple timelines and realities, and that time – past, present and future – can exist all at once. This is a concept that is very hard for the rational mind to accept. Could I be living multiple lifetimes now? It made sense, given my experiences.

As the weeks passed since 'the Jean effect' of opening me up to greater consciousness, I noticed I would often see what I would describe as 'twinkies'. Shiny bright purple objects in the corner of my eye. They were never there long enough to clearly discern as they would disappear the instant I recognised their presence. I only knew they were always purple and would appear randomly. The Egyptian glyphs also reappeared on a regular basis, as did the sacred geometry grids. They took on different themes, one of the most beautiful was a mixture of pinks and golds arranged in a heart-shaped crystal formation.

One night Cheri was having trouble sleeping, so I decided to massage her back to help her relax. Suddenly, my hands began to vibrate over her back, but this time there was no water or electricity involved. As I looked at the walls – still plastered with many hand symbols – the vibrating and pulsing in my hands became stronger. As I watched, the wall turned into a magical display of twinkling stars. Cheri fell asleep but, fascinated by what had occurred, I decided to lie down next to her and, eventually, I too went to the land of dreams.

A couple of hours later, I awoke to Cheri talking in her sleep, only she was speaking in a strange language I could not understand. As I comforted her by rubbing her back, I noticed my hands were once again vibrating. *How bizarre!* I rolled over and went back to sleep. From deep slumber I was awakened by the most hideous of sick headaches and thumping tinnitus. It was so bad I had to leave the room and escape to my own bed. It was like the vibration in the room was way too high for my human senses to handle, and once I was safely back in my own bed, the symptoms subsided.

More revelations were discovered with another weekend workshop, and a couple of days later my life became even stranger. My sleep began uneventfully, but at some time in the night I woke and became acutely aware that I could not identify my location.

In the pitch black, I reached over to turn on the bedside lamp, but could not feel it. I felt for the covers but they were not there, and neither was my pillow. I groped for the bedhead, curtains, window – anything of some sort of material existence – but there was nothing. Then I realised I did not have a body and I was floating somewhere in space. Only my mind was present, and even though I did not have a form, I still found myself trying to escape from what I still perceived as my bedroom.

My rational mind thought about escaping through the door, but my perception of the world was now only abstract as space and time had shifted. The walls and doors had all disappeared and I began to be fearful about how to retrieve my physical existence. I remember screaming out to my daughter for help. My cries were futile since I was no longer in her reality. Eventually, after floating above the abyss for a while, I noticed I could feel and sense my body returning. Not long after, the bed materialised as did the other items in the room. I sat up in bed in total darkness – confused and disorientated – and was about to turn on the light when I noticed the door leading to the hallway had disappeared, and in its place were what could only be described as four pillars of light.

I was awestruck by their shining magnificence and I stared at the shimmering silhouettes. They were beautifully golden and did not approach me; it was as if their loving energy was sufficient. After what seemed an eternity, they began to dematerialise and then vanished into what looked like a cloud of smoke.

What a trip! I thought, as I stumbled out of bed and turned on the light. Everything was in its rightful place, and the doors and walls were exactly as they should have been. *Where in the world did I go?*

I had only ever travelled out-of-body in my dreams, but this time was different and it seemed I had experienced interstellar travel. I felt I was out of the earthly matrix and could not find my way back. *But where did I go and who were the beings of light? Did they take me away and then return me safely to my bedroom and if so, what message were they conveying?*

So many questions!

Still in awe of what had transpired during the night, I set about my day. Then I noticed a new face had appeared on the window. Startled by the prominent features of the image: This one was definitely male and of human origin. It was vital and animated, as if it had been captured in a painting. I was studying the large eyes and prominent nose that stared at me. *Who are you? Are you the one who left the massive humanoid handprints or are you yet another bringer of knowledge?*

There was something familiar about his features – but I could not place it. The prominent nose might hold a clue. As a family, we all have well-proportioned noses; he could be a ghostly apparition of a past ancestor?

His long brown hair certainly suggested an ancient period; perhaps the Roman era. It was almost like he was beckoning me to talk with him, as his eyes followed me around the room.

After so many entities appearing and reappearing on my window, I had gotten quite comfortable with their presence. I decided to leave him whilst hoping for more insight.

I decided to lie down for a nap before attending a meeting in town. As I relaxed and allowed all worldly matters to dissipate, I began to feel some very strange bodily sensations. Instantly, the blur between my present reality and some past reality collided and I experienced the sensation of my aorta bursting and the life-giving blood drain away.

In another reality, I became aware that I was a soldier on the battlefield. I had taken a direct hit from an object I could not identify. In my present reality, I felt every sensation of the weapon and literally felt my guts and my aorta rip violently apart. "Oh my God!" I cried, as my mind screamed that I had just died. I moaned and as consciousness slipped away, I heard myself say, "I love you all."

Abruptly, I was back in the present and I frantically felt my abdomen for any evidence of a wound. Nothing. No injury, no masses of blood pouring from my body. *What the hell? Is that what it is like to die?* But, as I touched and pinched myself, I was real. *Did I just dream this death scene or did it really happen?* I was confused and unable to rationalise what just occurred. I can only say: If it was a dream then what is reality? The visceral and sensory aspects were just too intense to dismiss.

Many months later I still think about the experience and the impact it had on my life. I noticed the irrational fear of death I had experienced after my mother died – and the ongoing anxiety that prevailed – had subsided. I could now face the end of life, not so much from a negative aspect but with a sense of positive wonder about the next stage of the journey. I believe I was indeed that soldier in another lifetime, and I was being shown this experience to overcome yet another spiritual block. Further readings on past life regression led me to an understanding of quantum entanglement and the concept of different realities in different worlds. There is no past, present or future; they are all happening at once.

The concept of quantum reality really does my head in, but from a layman's point of view there are multiple copies of me in the Universe, living in different timelines, realities and dimensions. Every now and then these continuous lives may bump into each other in the form of entanglement. This makes sense to me as, with this experience – though I felt that I was living a past life – I was still firmly in the here and now. Yet I experienced it all as if it was one and the same – just like my car accident experience. It was like there were two of me in two different realities and we switched the program so the other reality copped the damage.

Whoa – what a ride! But wait – there is more! And all on the same day!

After this life-changing experience, I headed for the shower to get ready for my afternoon workshop. As I washed my hair, I was overpowered by a magnificent flash of purple light manifesting in front of me. It was such an intense shade of purple that I was momentarily dazzled. As quickly as it appeared, it vanished, leaving me perplexed. Had I actually witnessed this colourful display?

After drying my hair and dressing, I grabbed my keys and headed for the door. As I passed the sliding door, my eyes fell on the face of the Roman gladiator who once again held my gaze. I soon realised his expression had changed; his face no longer seemed to be holding a desire to speak to me. *I must remember to erase this image when I get home.* My mind was still millions of miles away thinking about the day's events.

My vestibular issues mean I do not like driving at the best of times, and this workshop was on the other side of town. I had myriad lights to stop at before reaching my destination. Intersections are particularly troublesome for me as, when the car comes to a complete stop, it is as if I am still moving because my balance struggles to maintain momentum – that visual illusion again. All was going well and I was handling the traffic relatively easily, when something disturbing happened.

I came to a standstill at a set of lights about five minutes from the venue. Feeling relatively relaxed, with my mind still on the matters of the day, anxiety over driving seemed well in the background. Then, as if some little gremlin had taken over my brain, my eyes rolled back into my head and I momentarily passed out. Thank God I was stationary as I could have easily had an accident. It was so fast, that before I could register what had happened, I was fully conscious when the lights turned green.

Panic set in. I was not sure whether to keep driving or pull over and wait to see if it happened again. Trembling violently, I managed to make it to the venue and downed some Valium. I have had anxiety and panic whilst driving before, but nothing like this had ever occurred. I decided to go inside and see if it happened again. The workshop's duration was two hours and everything was fine. I decided to drive home as it was now dark, and there was less sensory overload, with much less traffic. Again, nothing happened. But I diligently booked myself in for an MRI, just in case I was developing a brain tumour. Again, nothing sinister was discovered, but I found it strangely unnerving – as if some force had taken over my body.

I decided to erase my Roman friend from the window in the hope that this would end my *Alice in Wonderland* adventures. I also decided to contact my mentor, Jean Sheehan, to get her thoughts on the matter. After hearing about my adventures, it was obvious that I was changing timelines and that I had experienced what is known as 'zero point' consciousness. This meant I had returned to the source – or the oneness of the Universe. The NDE was also a shift in reality but in addition it was to enlighten me about an obviously significant past life.

But who was the face on the mirror? Was that actually me in a past existence? What was the force that seemed to enter my body? Did it have something to do with kundalini energy as I continued to open up to other worlds or was it just purely an anxiety attack? And the violet flash before my eyes? I had completed body electronics courses in previous years and I had read about St Germain and the violet flame. *Was this again a message of some kind that I needed to pay attention to?*

I was open to finding the answers to the clues and completing the puzzle. It would not be long before I would find the person who could solve the riddle of these bizarre and sometimes frightening experiences. I would finally get to know the answer to: **Who am I?**

CHAPTER SEVEN

My Starseed Origins

After such a stupendous ride, I again began to consider the possibility that my damaged brain had made all of this up in a series of hallucinations. But the evidence on the walls and mirrors was undeniable. *Why am I thinking this way?* I have always been very open to the possibilities of other realms and lifetimes. Suddenly it dawned on me: It was not so much about acknowledging these experiences, but more about fear and apprehension around the implications of this knowledge.

I had only told my closest friends about my escapades and, although open to the possibilities, they considered there was a perfectly rational explanation for my experiences. Other not-so-enlightened individuals viewed it all as 'a load of bullshit', which only served to ignite more fear and apprehension. I still had timeline shifts during the nocturnal hours, and the marching Bashar reminded me of my existence between worlds.

Since the luminous display of light beings in the hallway, the ensuing experiences were always only with one entity whose presence usually hovered in the doorway. On one particular night, however, I awakened to the familiar sight of golden light. But this time it created a majestic space in front of the entrance to the wardrobe and not from the exit. I seemed to struggle to find the way out as, once again, the walls and doors had all shifted. What happened next was something very difficult to convey in words.

I could no longer feel my physical self, and what can only be described as my 'light body' moved seamlessly through the silhouette that appeared directly in front of the wardrobe. I also sensed my little dog, who usually slept on the floor beside me, had also turned into a light body and faithfully followed behind me.

As in Narnia – The Lion, the Witch and the Wardrobe where the children began in one reality and entered another, since physicality no longer existed, I glided through the internal part of the wardrobe, and out the other side, my dog close behind. What happened after that I cannot recall, only that after some time I must have returned to the third-dimensional reality. There I found myself and my canine friend walking down the hallway where, now back in 'reality', I went to the toilet and then proceeded back up the hallway to walk through the re-emerged doorway. I lay down once again on the bed which only a few minutes ago did not exist. So mind-blowing!

Hungry for answers I began to research our galactic connections and all things alien. As I was busy trawling the internet for clues, I came upon a website that offered a Starseed astrology reading. Whatever is a Starseed? As discussed in the first chapter it appears Starseeds have not only had previous lives on planet Earth, but also other star systems and planets in other galaxies. As part of their soul contract, many have incarnated on Earth at this time to help raise the collective consciousness of Earth. The purpose of this mission is to hold the light and a higher vibration so others may awaken to their higher purpose.

As discussed in Chapter Two, the Starseed characteristics – a deep connection to all things metaphysical, a love of crystals and stones, having paranormal abilities and feeling the emotions of others – confirmed what I knew in my heart: This was me. The most profound characteristic however is having 'a deep sense of not belonging' and 'wanting to go home'. This truly resonated at my essence – my core. From my birth I had felt alienation from my siblings and an inability to connect to society's norms. This constant feeling of not belonging had haunted me and made it difficult to find acceptance. I felt a desperate urge to discover more. What galaxy do I come from? I enthusiastically entered my birth details and waited for the chart to arrive.

Well! It arrived – what a revelation!

All the strange happenings interwoven into my life now made perfect sense. From the faces on the mirror, hand imprints, strange symbols, Bashar, my lion/man – and even the craggy old duck! They all represented pieces of a jigsaw that had been solved. Finally.

Not only have I become aware of my galactic origins but also, as part of my Starseed origins, I have had many lifetimes in many galaxies. In my astrological chart is the constellation of Orion and the first revelation is that Orion is the home of the original Druids. Remember the face on the mirror that looked like a Roman? Perhaps this was to inform me of my ancestral roots of life as a Druid. My NDE not long after this face appeared also projected a time when I was in battle as a soldier.

Given my English and Welsh background, I believe I have had many lifetimes in conflict over lands and religion. Perhaps I was a Druid in one lifetime and was killed by a Roman soldier. Then, maybe in my next incarnation, my Roman self was replaced with that of a Druid in order to experience the duality of different life philosophies and to balance out karmic agreements.

Those who originate from Orion are closely aligned to Earth's moon. According to my Starseed astrological chart I have Moon in Gemini in the 8th house. Those originating from Orion are also masters at working with the duality of light and dark, hence my ability to still hold the light, even when these dark forces were infiltrating my home. They also have an amazing ability to translate galactic languages: The golden glyphs and symbols that were downloaded to me! They are also proficient at interdimensional travel: My ability to experience parallel universes and lucid dreaming.

One of the stars in the Orion constellation is Mintaka, which means 'belt' and forms part of Orion's Belt. I resonated deeply with this star as those of Mintakan heritage have a deep longing to go home. I never understood why this feeling was ever-present but now, for the first time, I knew.

Mintakan Starseeds have a difficult time with harsh and stressful environments and see the world through idealistic eyes. Therefore, due to their sensitive gentle natures, they can be easily used and abused by others. Although I have been bullied in this lifetime, as a Mintakan I take the view of 'what lessons can I learn from this experience?' and operate from a place of nonjudgement.

Those who are less forgiving find it extremely frustrating to be around Mintakans' energy. Some see them as being weak and inferior due to their non-linear way of approaching life. Part of the Mintakans' soul contract is to help others gain a more balanced approach to self, and to accept all aspects of themselves. This includes the shadow parts within, so they can be more aligned to the divine light and therefore reach their highest potential.

Mintakans love their homes and place beauty and creativity energies into their personal space. Perhaps this is why I mourned the loss of my beautiful home so deeply. Mintakan Starseeds also have a deep connection to water. Perhaps my irrational fear of deep water is one aspect of Mintakan life that I chose to forget. Is it too painful, or is there another unidentified reason? Perhaps the ability to vibrate with electricity and water is also part of my long-lost connection to this galactic ancestry.

Perhaps the most fascinating Starseed connection for me was to Regulus, The Royal Star of the North – also known as The Kingly Star – in the constellation of Leo (The Lion's Heart). I have Uranus and North Node in Leo in the 10th house. Regulus is a gateway, or portal, to other dimensions and is considered to be the original home of the fae (the fairy people): Nature spirits and unicorns. Regulus Starseeds are known for their love of nature and the elements, and the messages they receive from the other dimensions are often translated into creative pursuits such as writing and fashion. Being recipients of royal decree, they enjoy the finer aspects of life and have the ability to access success, fame and wealth with grace and dignity. Was Bashar, the lion/shaman, here to show me my divine roots in this galaxy? I often felt that he was the gatekeeper to the other worlds – a bridge between the sky and the earth.

As a lover of pretty things, I enjoy dressing in pastels and sparkly fairy tutus, even at the age of sixty. That Peter Pan innocence is very much alive inside, and the freedom to express my individuality is vital to me. Cheri and I once had a psychic artist sketch our profiles via her third eye. Staring back at me was a nymph-like creature with elfin ears and sparkling crystal blue eyes. Cheri was the consummate cherub, with chubby, rosy red cheeks.

There are four royal stars in the galaxy representing north, south, east and west. Each star is represented by one of four archangels – Michael, Raphael, Uriel and Gabriel – known as 'The Watchers'. These angelic beings are the guardians of Earth and can be called on in times of need to provide guidance and courage in the face of darkness.

Raphael represents the North Star (Regulus). He is the Angel of Healing, which explains my love of alternative medicine and the healing arts. He is represented by emerald green – my favourite colour. In fact, I painted most of my beautiful home in shades of green. I have always found it to be the most soothing colour as it represents calm and closeness to nature.

Raphael's name reverberated in my psyche. I remembered an experience I had long before any of this information had been revealed to me. I had grieved the loss of my beloved animals for so long, and now knowing they are safe and well in another dimension, I decided to start manifesting a new fur baby. What breed of cat this time? Long-haired breeds take quite a lot of grooming, so I decided on a shorthaired breed. As I searched the internet, it was not long before I was drawn to the chubby-cheeked and leonine features of the British Shorthair. With their beautiful copper-orange eyes and regal appearance a photograph of a gorgeous male specimen seemingly beckoned me to make him my screen saver. Each day I would stare at his stately face and imagine him being part of the household. I imagined what I would call this gorgeous specimen if I owned him and guess what? The name I came back to repeatedly was indeed Raphael!

Many years later I welcomed a cat of similar features into the household and he is Raphael. His nickname became Alfie-Duck in honour of the little duck! Not long after Raphael arrived, I purchased a female Brit called Luna, in honour of the moon, which I love so much. With her chubby round face and sorrowful eyes her feminine energy was the perfect accompaniment to Raphael's masculine energy. Ahh, the synchronicity of the universal flow. Yin and yang in perfect union: Think it and it will come.

One of the more controversial Starseed connections has been the reptilian creatures that invaded my home. I have wondered about these confronting entities. Galactic history says they are to be feared due to their war-mongering and lack of empathy. Many human hybrids choose not to embrace this particular ancestry, but I wanted to know.

Sure enough, there it was: Venus and Pluto in the 11th house is conjunct Draco.

Despite their dark past, it seems some wish to release the shackles that have bound their hearts and move away from fear to unconditional love. I believe that is why I am here: To make amends for the past and shine a light on the divide that keeps us apart.

Reptilian energy is practised at reading others and its proponents are highly observant. My emotional intelligence has never let me down. I have always felt the energies in my solar plexus immediately I meet someone. When I have ignored an uneasy feeling, it has always been to my detriment. Maybe they are also teaching me to find my voice and leadership skills, and not fear the consequences of those actions.

And what of the images of ribcages and vertebrae that appeared on the mirror? What was the message they were trying to convey? I have always had bone problems – particularly in the neck and upper thoracic region – with constant constriction in the muscles. It is almost as if this aspect of my anatomy does not fit properly inside my human skeletal frame.

And having RH negative blood may hold a clue too. RH negative blood is known as dragon- or lizard-blood, and one of the characteristics is an extra rib – which I have.

Medical intuition teaches that bones are where your deepest core values lie and are the beginning of the framework of your life. Perhaps I have created stories in my life that were not true to my authentic self. I did not back myself and, instead of seeing the experience as part of the lessons of life and integrating that into my belief system, I chose to hold those painful memories in my connective tissue. This made muscles rigid and unresponsive to change. Perhaps the flute symbols left on the ceiling were another attempt to communicate the need to relax and simply go with the universal flow so that new experiences could be created effortlessly.

The other two Starseed lineages, although not quite as significant – but still important – are Alpha Centauri and Pleiades. Scorpio in the 1st house of Quantum Light Body is conjunct Alpha Centauri. Centaurians are avid seekers of spiritual knowledge. They are easily drawn to departed spirits and angelic beings. Is this why I attract visitations from spirits such as my father, mother and brother?

Centaurians are multifaceted thinkers and do not box themselves into a limited understanding of the Universe. I can relate to this concept since I have been ridiculed for my ideas around medicine, the way I dress and my unorthodox approach to living. When I have a strong opinion on a subject I am passionate about, I am not easily swayed and will hold steadfast to my truth. However, I accept this is not always the truth of others and that as I learn and grow, my perception may change.

The final Starseed lineage is Pleiades. This is a group of stars known as The Seven Sisters. Conjunct Pleiades in my star chart is the Descendant in Taurus in the 7th house. There are many Pleiadeans here on Earth now. Their task is to raise the consciousness of humanity from our materialistic 3D existence to the higher 5D vibration of unconditional love. They are highly intuitive and empathic due to their open-hearted energy. They like to be of service to others – my gravitation towards the healing arts.

I had heard of 'light language' having experienced many cosmic downloads of symbols and grids; however, I had never actually spoken the language. You will recall I had witnessed Cheri speaking in a strange tongue when I slept with her after the car-bashing incident had frightened her. I had awakened to a strange extremely irritating humming sound. The loudness and frequency induced my consequent excruciating migraine, nausea and tinnitus. It meant I could not stay in her room another second. As soon as I returned to my own bedroom the noise subsided and, with my headache dissipating, I was able to fall asleep. What had transpired that night? What was the strange language that Cheri was speaking? Not long after, totally unaware of my actions, my husband told me I had conversed in my sleep for about five minutes in an unknown language.

I decided to search the internet for videos with Starseeds speaking in their light languages and presented a series of voices to him that may have been similar to the one in which I had spoken. It was not long before he picked out one he thought was a replica of my strange utterances. Of course, it was the light language of the Pleiadeans. More interesting, after hearing it myself, I realised it was the same language spoken by Cheri during that eventful night. Cheri had her chart read and it seems that Pleiades and Orion are our shared connections. Makes sense given our paranormal experiences and our shared reptilian bloodline.

CHAPTER EIGHT

The Puzzle is Complete

I needed to have a more in-depth review of my Starseed chart. It was not long before a lovely soul, Donna Diane, contacted me. Donna Diane is the astrologer who put my chart together and, because it was so interesting, she felt compelled to offer me a complimentary consultation to discuss her findings.

My first Starseed lineage is from the constellation Orion. Donna Diane explained that Orion is the home of the original Druids, hence the Roman on the window to remind me of my ancestral roots. My Celtic ancestors are from south east England, particularly the county of Kent, on the same longitude as the Michael Ley Line which traverses Glastonbury. This ley line – named after Archangel Michael – contains a vortex of energy which links up to various historical sites including Tintagel Castle, and Merlin's Cave; Merlin, the great wizard, would take his initiates to Tintagel, believed to be King Arthur's birthplace. It is thought these ley lines line up with Orion's Belt. The stars in the belt comprise: Alnitak, Alnikm and Mintaka. Mintaka, of course, is another one of my Starseed origins.

Donna Diane then proceeded to my Draco lineage. Many people are in denial of this part of our galactic history as it is perceived that due to the Reptilians' lust for power and control over other planetary systems, they are only of the dark side. There are some Reptilians, however, who wanted to increase their level of consciousness to acquire a more enlightened existence and be of service to humanity. The more positive aspects of the Reptilian energy are leadership and being able to hold your own power. In other words, not following the crowd and being a critical thinker.

I have always been 'the black sheep of the family' and 'a free thinker', so can easily relate to this concept. With this powerful dragon energy comes the ability to be comfortable with both the dark and the light as part of the duality of all things. Curiously, I have never been unduly afraid of the creepy reptilian images that showed up in the house nor of their paranormal antics. I now understand their showing up was all part of the plan to awaken me to all aspects of my being – the good and the bad. Reptilians also have the special ability to shapeshift through various timelines and dimensions; it had become obvious to me that I possess this ability.

As my Moon in Gemini is connected to Mercury in Scorpio in the 12-house – known as The House of the Unseen – I am easily able to connect with the dark and the light forces. Sometimes, however, weird crazy thoughts may enter my mind; these may, in fact, be those of others. For example, not listening to my intuitive self and throwing away the obsidian left under the car. They were meant for protection against such intrusions. Scorpio ruled by Pluto is connected to the planet Neptune which acts as an antenna, and Mercury amplifies the energy. Being closely aligned to Mercury, I am like a tuning fork for all types of incoming energy. Therefore, it is imperative to cleanse what is not mine.

Donna Diane, working with her spiritual guides, suggested I utilise the stone fire quartz to help with intergalactic communication, and to act as a shield and protector whilst I worked with both negative and positive entities.

I also have Venus in Virgo – a sign of the goddess.

The goddess energy teaches us not be afraid of the dark, and shows a way to walk in the dark. I also have Pluto in Virgo, otherwise known as The Destroyer or Transformer of Energy. Since I have been chosen to show the way for the new spiritual consciousness, I must be brave enough to use this feminine energy to destroy and transmute negativity, in order to create heaven on earth. I feel certain now that some of the symbols left on the ceiling by interdimensional beings – in particular the wavy flute-like lines – are a representation of the yin (feminine) and yang (masculine), energy as it aligns to the balance of universal light and darkness. 'Go with the flow of life' being its mantra.

I have never been sure of my exact birthtime but, through working with her guides, Donna Diane felt sure I was born at 8.22am. In numerology, the number 8 is the sign of infinity, related to power and success; and the number 22 is about creativity and intuition. According to the astrological chart, this birthtime also connects me to the constellation of Taurus, which comprises the Seven Sisters of Pleiades. These seven stars are also known as the seven Hathors – goddesses that reside over the tombs in ancient Egypt and provide sustenance to their worshippers.

As Pleiadean Starseeds are here to assist humanity with the ascension process, it is imperative I keep my heart chakra open to both the masculine and feminine energies. In doing so, I can help balance this energy in others and open myself up to telepathic connections, lucid dreaming and prophetic dreams. I am grateful for the communication through the Pleiadean light language, and the gift of the ability to speak to departed loved ones, and to know of future events through the dream state.

The other important Starseed origin for me is Regulus under the constellation of Leo (otherwise known in Arabic as 'The Heart of the Lion'). Regulus is part of a fixed star system with four stars pertaining to the four kings, or our four archangels mentioned earlier, known as 'The Watchers'. They are known as the guardians of the sky. Their brightness denotes them as royalty and they hold the four aspects of the Universe together. We already know these archangels: they are Aldebaran (Michael: 'Who is Like God', in the east in the Taurus constellation); Regulus (Raphael: 'God's

Remedy', in the north in the Leo constellation); Antares (Uriel: 'God's My Light', in the west in the Scorpio constellation) and Fomalhaut (Gabriel: 'God's Strength', in the south in the Pisces constellation).

I believe Raphael to be my guardian angel; he is known as the healing angel and is central to the evolvement of my interest in alternative medicine and healing modalities. The constellation of Leo – the Lion – is an important representative of strength and honour of the night sky. Hence, my beautiful Bashar, my other protector and guardian, has come to 'wake me up'. As a Regulus Starseed I am also attuned to the elements of nature and the magical life of the fairies, pixies and unicorns. Some personal items, including my favourite fairy dress and my numerology book, have disappeared. Is it the impish pixies who are taking them? Or have I taken them to my other lives in other realities?

Regulus is an interdimensional bridge to other galaxies and is the home of the shaman. Bashar, my shaman, shows me how to cross into the other realities.

According to my chart, I have Uranus conjunct Regulus which moves through a sign every 2,160 years. However, something very profound happened to my chart in 2011. Regulus moved to zero degrees of Virgo, which announced a merging of the divine masculine and divine feminine energies. I firmly believe I experienced 'the dark night of the soul' and, as this was such a traumatic event, I almost feel I swapped souls – my 'walk-in'.

In January 2020 there was a conjunction of Saturn and Pluto in Capricorn, which was exactly conjunct my natal Saturn. The last time these two planets were conjunct in Capricorn was in the early 1500s. Donna Diane asked if anything profound happened to me during this time or a few months later. After deliberating, I realised this is when I began my journey into the world of medical intuition and the repatterning of the DNA, opening me up to the potentiality of the Universe. I then realised my own NDE represented the dawning of this new Saturn return, and the end of the old Earth we know, and has ushered in the new Age of Aquarius. Donna Diane said the gridding techniques shift at a very deep level and this is when I shared with her the family patterning.

You see, we have a genetic lung condition which was unknown to the family for many years. When my mentor, Jean, looked into my body she described an ancient lineage of clairvoyants and healers. Throughout the ages such a practice was forbidden and the energetic imprint changed. Metaphysically they were told to 'get rid of it' and 'hide it in the back of the lung'. I was also told by Donna Diane that Gemini, which is very strong in my chart, rules the lungs.

Donna Diane had also said that the sign of Leo in my chart represents a legacy and is a unique energy. The sign of Leo is something you birth; this explains my coming back from the future to be here now. Donna Diane also feels strongly that it is connected with communication, perhaps writing a book, or leaving some type of elixir for people simply by shaking their hand. I know my hands pulse when I hold the hand of others, so perhaps that is the gift Archangel Raphael has endowed me. Donna Diane pointed to 'the elixir' as a series of ancient codes the other person may or may not be aware of, depending on their level of consciousness. Either way a healing exchange is taking place.

Donna Diane also found my experiences with water and electricity fascinating. She said it felt as if this electrical energy surge is repeatedly jolting Gaia as I walk on the earth. She likened it to an energy reboot and, in her words 'leaving the elixir of flowers wherever I step'. Flowers represent the divine feminine and, through their beautiful sacred geometry, bring a sense of joy and wonder to the world. I would like to think that this 'flower energy' somehow helps to raise the consciousness of the world to help create a community of connectedness.

According to Donna Diane, my Moon in Gemini have past life connections to ancient Egypt and the Anunnaki, or 'sky people' who visited the earth and created a hybridised race of humans. This explains my RH negative blood. One of these ancient deities – known as Thoth in Egypt and Hermes in Greece – and was also proposed to be the reincarnation of St Germain. He is an ascended master whose gift of the violet flame can transmute lower vibrational energies.

I had a lightbulb moment! This is the same St Germain I learned about in the body electronics course I attended all those years ago. This was where the experience of transmutation led me to have the extraordinary episode of my upper back and ribs realigning. The ultimate aim of the course was to remove all obstacles to such enlightenment so one may experience the kundalini fire and, ultimately, the violet flame to bring about death of old negative beliefs and a rebirth of a more enlightened self. Ah ha! The death process on the bed came to mind, along with the big purple flash that overcame me in the shower.

Donna Diane also spoke about my Moon in Gemini having past life connections to my Sun in Libra, and having an Aquarius connection. Although I have past lives as royalty, there is also the humanitarian who yearns to balance the scales of injustice. The Sun also holds my deepest wounding of the divine feminine. My South Node is connected to Chiron, known in astrology as 'the wounded healer'. In a past life, I have experienced the deepest wound. I had fallen to my knees and cried out to God asking why he had forsaken me. Donna Diane believes this has happened around the time of the fall of Atlantis but, due to the Aquarius connection, may also be associated with the twin flame separation I know so well. Like the time I was opened up in a medical intuitive session and cried like a wounded animal reliving some sort of past trauma.

On reflection, I think it was about having to return to planet Earth and not wanting to go through the birth canal. But maybe I was experiencing the horror of Atlantis and my drowning. As explained in previous chapters, my fear of water is ever-present. Donna Diane also alluded to an eclipse, where a person from my past will re-enter my life to heal the situation. I will be watching for this with bated breath. She also spoke of heightened sensors during this time, with psychic and sensory experiences at full amplitude.

My reading with Donna Diane was in 2019 – the year the world stopped due to the menacing presence of the Covid-19 pandemic. How a virus could change our entire way of life is mind-boggling. It continues still. Prior to its onslaught on our psycho/socio/economic environment, I had become increasingly dismayed by the fast-paced existence that humans had created for themselves. No time to 'smell the roses' as our desire to 'keep up with the Joneses' has kept us like a hamster on a wheel. Enslaved to the almighty dollar to pay for huge mansions and the latest gadget, work/life balance was perilously unbalanced. One missed mortgage payment, an incapacitation or illness, would be the death knell to such a lifestyle. What would happen to those of us unfortunate enough not to have even the basic human needs of food and shelter? The gap between the rich and poor widened.

Then one day everyone was told to retreat to their homes, and the economy ground to a halt. I remember it. The world fell eerily quiet. Deserted streets and buildings, not a car in sight, just the pigeons going about their usual business. The great spiritual awakening had begun.

I had felt for some time that the planet was in the process of a deep cleanse. First there were the fires that roared over the Australian bush in December 2018, and now – without humans pillaging the environment on a daily basis – many species of plants and animals were able to make a resurgence with smog-free air and fresh, unpolluted water. The homeless were given an opportunity to get off the streets and into comfortable accommodation, a luxury rarely afforded those in true need.

Humans were forced to work from home and spend much needed time with family, creating a space for creativity. I was very grateful for the opportunity to step out of the world for a time and concentrate further on spiritual self-development. I undertook Reiki and crystal healing courses, as well as women's circle facilitation. I thoroughly enjoyed the experiences, but felt there was another course out there I was destined to undertake. It was not long before my mentor, Jean Sheehan, contacted me to offer a place in her Modern Medicine Woman retreat. I accepted without hesitation, and would find yet another piece of the puzzle that would consolidate and affirm all that I had come to know.

The retreat was held in autumn, with cool, crisp air, and majestic mountains of the Sunshine Coast hinterland as a backdrop. Dressed in my Medicine Woman outfit, I felt relaxed and eager to mix with like-minded souls. On the first evening we began journaling in anticipation of our 'vision quest' the following evening. Jean explained the purpose of the vision quest was to make a connection with a spirit animal. This creature would then take you on a guided journey of initiation, in order to claim your rite of passage to be bestowed the title of queen or goddess.

Each day we were asked to ponder a question. From my notes, this is what I wrote each day, as I claimed my Starseed lineage. This was the first time that I had ever written down my experience, and it was a revelation to see how much the written word resonated.

This is what I know to be true – day 1

> *I am a multidimensional being who has jumped timelines to be here on this earth at this time.*
>
> *I come in the form of a Starseed goddess as part of the awakening and shift in consciousness.*
>
> *To be the light and way-shower for others.*
>
> *I am reserved but resilient providing unconditional love to all.*
>
> *I hold space for others and reach out my hand in loving kindness for each has their own path in life.*
>
> *I am a sentient being who experiences the world through feelings, sensations, colour, tones and imagination.*
>
> *I dislike harshness and find it difficult to ground to planet Earth. I have an affinity with water and electricity with the combination creating resonance within my body.*

If you were an animal, what would you be and why – day 1

> *I would be a lion.*
>
> *The lion comes to me through a mirror. He sometimes morphs into an Indigenous shaman that I have called Bashar.*
>
> *I have sketched him. He has come to wake me up to my ancestral lineage and to be a bridge between worlds.*
>
> *He is from the Royal Star Regulus reminding me of my Starseed lineage with the fae.*
>
> *He is my protector and guide into the other dimensions.*
>
> *Bashar offers freedom and independence – 'born free'.*

> *I sometimes ask to go see him and, in my dreams, he responds by downloading a grid to help me see in my mind's eye.*
>
> *This grid provides hidden knowledge that I still do not understand.*
>
> *I want to roar like the lion!*
>
> *I am meek but brave and powerful.*
>
> *I am the Lionheart.*

What do I know to be true this morning – day 2

> *My energy was supercharged as I felt the power of the Earth surging through my hands in synchronisation with my heartbeat.*
>
> *A sliding picture show in my mind took me to a past life with 1900s motor cars against a backdrop of horses and carriages.*
>
> *The Universe welcomed me with a kaleidoscope light-show of swirls and fractals.*
>
> *As the moon and stars in all their silvery glory melted into my mind, I became one with all there is.*

We were now prepared for our vision quest by lying down on our mats and being tucked up in blankets as if in a sarcophagus. Before entering my tomb, I glanced out at the most splendiferous moon that seemed to summon my attention. As I stared at its solitary embrace, I was overcome with such a powerful emotion I began to quiver and shake all over. A deep feeling of sadness and aloneness threatened to derail my vision quest before I had even contemplated such a journey. With tears rolling down my cheeks and still shaking uncontrollably, I managed to pull myself away from the magnetic attraction of the moonlight.

Once tucked safely in my cocoon, my emotional reaction settled as we listened to the instructions regarding travelling with our spirit animal. We were to summon the animal and walk with it to the mountains in the far distance. I remember being with Bashar but, before I knew it, I found my body in a rhymical thrusting action as if my spirit was about to take flight. That is all I can remember as I seemed to travel at warp speed up into the galaxy.

After what seemed like just a short time, we were called back to our physical body. I wanted to stay wherever I had been travelling to, and was not particularly excited about returning. In discussions with the other goddesses, it seemed everybody had interdimensional experiences whether they be on the earthly plane or in spiritual realms. But my travels seemed more intergalactic. Instead of feeling accepted within the tribe, I felt more alone than ever, as it was becoming apparent that no-one else had experienced any Starseed connections.

The next morning, I felt the most intense homesickness. The 'wanting to go home' feeling overcame me. Jean showed me photos of 'the dudes' that were present at the ceremony and, although comforting, I was drawn to the sight of a huge bolt of lightning illuminating the night sky.

"Oh my gosh! That's the same bolt of lightning that was in my vision quest!"

Jean reassured me that I had both a purpose and a reason for being there and that there were other lost Starseeds out there wanting connection. She said, "This Starseed wisdom needs to be told so that others like you do not feel so alone and can embrace their own unique abilities."

I then excitedly told the others not only of my vision quest but also my unfolding journey as a Starseed.

This is what I know to be true – day 3

> *In my vision quest, Bashar my lion animal took me home to the constellation of Orion – the home of the original Druids. The Draco energy of my reptilian ancestry raises me as I soar out of the cocoon on dragon's wings.*
>
> *My lion acts as the protector and gatekeeper in partnership with the fae and the elementals. Archangel Raphael, as part of the Watchers in the North and the Elhoim, oversees*

my travels and reminds me of my connections to Regulus, Alpha Centauri, Pleiades and Mintaka.

I hold the resonance from my Druid past through the grids. I see Merlin, the great wizard, in my mind's eye. He uses his staff to create a great flash of electrical energy through the cosmos and beyond.

My lion shows me by just holding the resonance I can find what I need on Mother Earth and all that I touch with this resonance will know love.

I was given a sword charged with the energy of the moon to bring back down to Mother Earth.

I am told, under the principle of the four elements, my resonance carries the electrical charge. I now understand how these four elements, together with the five-element theory in Chinese philosophy, relate to the context of my journey.

- ★ *Earth: Archangel Uriel grounds the earth energies.*
- ★ *Metal: the sword holds the electrical charge of the earth.*
- ★ *Wood: used in the guise of a little ornament resemblant of a wood duck to open a portal to bring through the ancient wisdom of the codes of existence and the alchemy of transformation to create heaven on earth. Wood duck meaning: ducks fly in the air onto the earth and water below. As above so below.*
- ★ *Fire: Archangel Michael guides the dragon passion for courage, strength and leadership. Fuelled by the wooden duck to create fire and ash (stardust) on the earth.*
- ★ *Air: Archangel Raphael guides the extra-dimensionals and the ethers.*
- ★ *Water: Archangel Gabriel guides the resonance with all the other elements creating the electrical charge for emotional upliftment and conscious universal flow.*

> *What do I need to tell my spirit animal?*
>
> *Thank you, Bashar, for showing me the way. I take my sword now and charge it with light.*

What I know to be true – day 4

> *I am a multidimensional goddess queen.*
>
> *I have been opened to all possibilities.*
>
> *I am releasing the armour that has shielded my heart and picked up my sword in honour of all those that have gone before me and all those that I will touch in the future.*
>
> *Shining bright with love and light.*

What a deliciously amazing time I had at the retreat! And what a gift of knowledge had been bestowed upon me. Although metaphorical in its expression, the vision quest had finally given me the tools to solve the puzzle of my journey into the unseen worlds. I can at last feel at peace with all I have encountered, content with the revelation that I am indeed a multidimensional being with extra-terrestrial lineage. The challenge now is to bring forth all that potentiality into the 3D earthly existence.

Some months had passed since the retreat and as I became more familiar with the retrogrades, eclipses and moon cycles, along came the Lionsgate 8/8 portal. As you know, the number eight represents infinity, and is a chance to break through all the limitations holding us back, and crash through any barriers standing in our way. Well, talk about crashing through! As I lay asleep, I was abruptly awoken by the sound of smashing glass.

I bounded out of bed and checked all the windows and glass doors, including glasses and crockery. Nothing broken. Cheri also heard the almighty ruckus and came to investigate. 'Break through the barriers', kept infiltrating my mind as I realised a new portal of opportunity had just opened.

In the next few weeks, I had boundless energy for all things spiritual. I purchased hundreds of beautiful stones and rocks, went back to creative art, made geometric grids, practised my meditations daily and generally felt a sense of bliss and peace. My mind kept wandering to Donna Diane's suggestion of writing a book and, before I knew it, I found myself thinking about the process and getting words onto paper.

Initially, I decided to write my memoir and two years later have completed the task. My dudes do not come to visit as often, but I know they are still around, encouraging me to achieve my highest potential every day. As my throat chakra has always been a stumbling block for me expressing myself, I was reminded of picking up my sword to all possibilities. I decided to make short videos to encourage my voice to be heard.

Sometimes, in a live shoot, I would start to falter and my voice would begin to quiver, but I would find the strength to overcome my hesitancy. During one such filming I was really struggling but after I faltered, miraculously, it turned out to be one of my best clips. As I was replaying the recording, my heart skipped a beat. I noticed in the corner a tiny fairy-winged creature dart by, and in another corner an orb of light flashed from one end of the room to the other. "Oh my God," I cried, "the fae are here spurring me on." Another time when I was stuck for words, a flash of magnificent light – akin to a shooting star – appeared on the ceiling. 'Shoot for the Stars' was the message and I gained inspiration to write from the heart. I also began practising automatic writing in order to have another channel of communication with other realms.

As I sank deep into my meditative state, I began scribbling the words received.

'Your special wisdom seer message', I deciphered intuitively from the scrawled scratching in front of me. With the words special meaning unique; wisdom having greater perception, and seer being someone who sees higher truth, I interpreted this message invited me to portray my own unique perception to the world with the insight of my higher truth. Such a profound statement that emanates from source or the authentic self.

Although Bashar no longer makes his appearance known on the window or through a theatrical dance on the roof, I know that I can call on him at any time for assistance. The house, although now relatively quiet, would occasionally open up a portal via the bathroom mirror or through Cheri's *Game of Thrones* sigil.

Mostly, soft feminine hands would appear. They looked decidedly human, although the occasional alien appendage would emerge, particularly in Cheri's room. We are now graced with two images of reptilian beings appearing in a stance of unification. Perhaps this depicts a signature of non-duality. Not good or bad, right or wrong, each being part of the whole to form a symbol of togetherness.

The retreat had also taught me I must value myself more, so I am organising a grand 60th birthday celebration! No small thing, as my brain tries to sabotage my thinking. I shall hold out my hand and be prepared to receive gifts of spontaneity, fun and joy.

As I conclude my adventures on this day – 11/1/2022 – I would like to think that these writings, although no doubt farcical for some, might inspire other Starseeds out there. If you have not yet connected to your roots and yet firmly know, somehow, you do not quite fit within the earthly way of life, the 11/1 portal is an opening to new beginnings, and 2022 represents completion. So, out with the old and in with the new way of thinking. Embrace these energies and you may just discover there is more to our existence than you could ever imagine. Our job is to bring forth that potentiality to the world so we can one day acknowledge our true existence, and be in constant communion with our galactic family. Never has there been a greater time to embrace our shared humanity, compassion and joy so we may all come together as part of the Law of One. Love and light and blessings to all.

A message from my intergalactic friends who channelled to me the writings of Sir Walter Scott whilst walking through a labyrinth maze at the retreat.

> *What a tangled web we weave*
> *When we are first open to deceive*
> *You will cast a spell and the*
> *truth will tell*

This is my interpretation of the meaning: "Deceived by our ego and thoughts, that we are somehow separate from the Divine. Truth is revealed when we awaken to the absolute power within. There is no illusion of separation only the awareness of the now and all there is – which is love."

Conclusion

I hope you enjoyed my ride of self-discovery and through the process have realised that you have your own unique story to tell. The hardest part for me in being different is finding authentic connections to others who also 'get it'. It is, therefore, important that, as like-minded souls, we reflect on the attributes of the Starseed lineages expressed in this book, such as:

- ★ *Gratitude*
- ★ *Simplicity*
- ★ *Harmony*
- ★ *Joy*
- ★ *Beauty*

So that we may all come together and be inspired from the heart.

My darling Pearl passed at 12.01 am (1+1+2) = 4 on the 10.06.2022 (1+6+2+2+2 = 13) 1+3 = 4. On the 13th June at 2.11 am (2+1+1) = 4. I lay restless in bed when the room seemed to become illuminated by a light outside my window. Bugger! The neighbours have left their porch light on. I reluctantly got up to ensure the curtains were completely drawn. It was then that I became awestruck by a super moon glowing in all its resplendence.

As I settled back to sleep I realised the curtain was still open and as I lay there contemplating whether I would get up again, I became entranced by an ethereal substance coming from the reflection of the moon. Its luminous silvery presence had created a portal effect straight down to the floor where my fur baby had passed.

The number four, in spiritual terms, is all about the heartspace. I would like to think that the moon goddess had called to the spirit of this little divine Starseed. She gently released her back to the Universe and all that is – which is love.

Goodbye my little friend. In my dreams I will enter the wardrobe and see you once again.

Pearl

About the Author

I am a naturopath and bodyworker with over thirty years' experience. 'Feel Good the Functional Way' is my motto for good health and wellbeing. From gut health to hormone health, I utilise functional medicine principles to identify and treat imbalances that lead to ongoing health issues.

Have you gone to the doctor only to be told that your blood tests are normal? That you are perfectly healthy and there is no explanation for the ongoing malaise and fatigue that seems to prevent you from living your best life?

Do you take the time to cook for yourself and understand the implications of what you eat on a daily basis? Are you partaking in regular exercise and enjoying the great outdoors? Are you immersing in all that nature has to offer? Stress is a killer of so much joy and happiness in life. It is therefore important to recognise negative self-talk and meditate daily.

How do you talk to your body? Do you hold onto resentment, anger and frustration and in what way do these negative emotions affect your organs and energy systems of the body? Perhaps you have bladder problems because you are `pissed off' with life or bowel problems because you are not digesting life and are hanging onto toxicity.

Health is not just about the physical symptoms but the unconscious thoughts and patterns we create to keep us in a state of less optimal health and vitality. My tool kit of intuitive readings, chakra stone balancing and pendulum readings can identify these imbalances and help reconstruct new and healthy ways of thinking.

The Butterfly Connection

Emergence of the Wise Goddess Within

Over 50s Women's Circle

★ *A place for contemplation and reflective thought*

★ *Sharing creative ideas*

★ *Social interaction and building friendships*

★ *Storytelling and ritual*

★ *Spirituality and energy healing*

★ *Fun and play*

Do you feel alone or misunderstood in the world? Have you ever considered joining a circle of like-minded individuals or starting a circle of your own? Come and join a circle with me.

What is a women's circle?

It is a gathering to reflect upon the principles of living an authentic life. I create a safe space of gratitude, simplicity, harmony, joy and beauty in a loving, nurturing environment. We share an intention to celebrate each other from the heart.

Who is it for?

This women's circle is ideal for you if you are a woman over 50 and are feeling as though something is missing from your life, you are in search for 'what next', you want authentic connection and to open your mind to new experiences.

For more information about the women's circle, naturopathy appointments or speaking engagements, please contact me:

Webpage: www.desleylocknaturopath.com.au

Email: desleylocknaturopath@outlook.com

Facebook: naturopathtoowoomba

Additional Resources

www.celestialblueprint.com

www.millenniumeducation.com

Cherub Cherish   *Elfin Queen Desley*

> "Break out of the cocoon you've built over the years with your fears and self-imposed restrictions. The world is waiting to savour you and all that you have to offer."

—GIA

www.ingramcontent.com/pod-product-compliance
Lightning Source LLC
Chambersburg PA
CBHW050254120526
44590CB00016B/2345